Pilgrimage of Love

PREMYATRA

Pilgrimage of Love
Book I

Swami Shri Kripalvanandji

Copyright © 1992
by Kripalu Yoga Fellowship

All Rights Reserved.
No portion may be reprinted without written
permission of Kripalu Yoga Fellowship.

"Kripalu" is a registered trademark
of Kripalu Yoga Fellowship.

First Printing 1981
Second Printing 1982
Third Printing 1988
Fourth Printing 1992

Printed by Kripalu Yoga Fellowship
P.O. Box 793, Lenox, MA 01240

Library of Congress
Catalog Card Number: 81-82015
ISBN: 0-940258-02-1 (Book I)
ISBN: 0-940258-06-4 (4 Volume Set)

My Beloved Gurudev,

    Whatever I have received
        —with Your grace—
On my pilgrimage
    to Your holy, lotus feet,
I dedicate to You.
    Obeisances. Your child,
        Kripalu

Contents

Preface vii
Chapter 1 Celibacy 1
Chapter 2 Nonviolence 21
Chapter 3 Truth 39
Chapter 4 Nonstealing 53
Chapter 5 Nonattachment 67
Glossary 81
Index 83

Preface

When I first arrived in America, I had been practicing the vow of silence for nineteen years. But, for the first three months after my arrival here, I spoke all day, every day. So, after having been silent for so long, Sister Tongue experienced difficulty. She would stutter and babble from time to time like a toddler stumbles while walking. Moreover, Honorable Brother Mind was also experiencing difficulty, and my thought flow was not very systematic. So, trying to speak was like trying to start up an old rusty machine. This confusion lasted three days, but then I slowed down my speech, and it improved.

The audiences were full of very accepting disciples and spiritual seekers who listened to me faithfully; although, naturally, they could not very well detect my difficulties, since I was not speaking their native language. In any event, gradually during the week, my train began running on its track.

While in America, I have been living in the two ashrams of Amrit Desai where 200 brother and sister disciples live. Groups of 250 to 500 or even 1,000 nonresident disciples also have been continually pouring in to participate in an ongoing schedule of programs lasting a day, a week, two weeks, a month, or a year.

To me, both ashrams are like lands of austerity and pilgrimage; or, from another perspective, they are supportive environments which promote mental and physical health. They have an atmosphere which fosters meditation and spiritual practices, and so it touches the hearts of all. Here, no one needs to seek peace—she comes on her own accord to welcome each person at the door.

The dual theme of yoga and devotion is emphasized throughout this text of discourses, and between these I have woven the principles of jnana, or knowledge. I have tried to remain vigilant to make the discourses helpful to seekers of various stages at all times; so I am fully confident that any sincere spiritual seeker will receive the guidance he desires, whether he is a beginning, intermediate, or advanced student of yoga. Moreover, since I selected some of the topics discussed, and the seekers have selected others, the text contains material of interest to a wide range of individuals.

Two main volumes constitute *Premyatra:* book one on the Science of Yoga and book two on the Science of Devotion. Book one contains three categories of discourses: spiritual disciplines and practices (yamas and niyamas), yoga, and informal conversations. These discourses focus equally upon the theoretical and practical aspects of growth. I have tried to guide seekers toward integrating spiritual practices into their personal, familial, societal, and national interactions, while remembering the principle that yoga can never be practiced by segregating life and religion. This focus is, in fact, a proper step in the overall sequence of human development. Book one concludes with a series of informal conversations with groups of disciples that include my answers to their questions.

To me, these sessions comprise a separate type of discourse, since they primarily involve introductory-level questions about yoga, devotion, and psychology. I have answered these from a general viewpoint, and, so, I have not organized them into chapters according to the specific topic area discussed.

Book two comprises four categories of discourses on the science of devotion: devotion to the Lord, the art of loving, bhajans or devotional songs, and kirtans or celebrative chants. These discourses focus on our relationships in everyday life and include affective commentaries on the bhajans and kirtans pertaining especially to the feelings conveyed. I have tried to make these discourses and commentaries emotionally expressive, scientifically sound, worthwhile reading, and fit for meditation. I have also given an extensive explanation of the practice of idol worship and have shown its usefulness to spiritual seekers.

I have made extensive use of anecdotes to illustrate principles discussed in the discourses. Lively anecdotes like "Vasavdatta meets Upgupatta," "The Slave and the Lion," and "Dala Tarvadi," are focused on the principle I wish to illustrate rather than merely on overly flamboyant and sentimental stories. I hope that this will facilitate recalling both the anecdote and its principle.

I flew from Bombay to New York City on May 20, 1977. These two volumes include nearly all my public discussions. They do not include my informal conversations during my first few days in America, since these were simply the talk of reunited loved ones. I consider the first day of discourses to be May 24, 1977, when I presented a brief affective commentary on the topic of kirtan.

All the discourses were transcribed by my dear disciple Dushyantkumar Patel of Ashi, India. Immediately after each session, he transcribed the tapes and put the transcripts into manuscript form. He concentrated solely on this task for many long days and nights. His efforts produced 800 pages of "clean copy" and an equal number of rough-draft pages. Additionally, he wrote a brief account of my travels in North America and correlated that travelogue into his manuscript. I have adapted the pertinent portion here, with the remainder to be published as a separate book entitled *Reminiscences of Premyatra: Prologue*.

My eyes filled with tears when I heard about Dushyantkumar's ideal and unforgettable service. He has performed this secret service as his sacred duty, never disclosing it to anyone. His dedication has touched my heart. His love and skill are clearly evident in the way he has incorporated details. Although he is not trained in writing, he has written nicely, and to the best of his ability. I give him my auspicious blessings.

As I researched, revised, and expanded the original manuscript transcribed by Dushyantkumar, it became all marked up. My dear disciple and aide, Vinit Muni, then prepared a "clean copy." He mentioned to me, "After Dushyantkumar left America, I also began writing a travelogue." Vinit Muni's travel notes will be published as a separate book entitled *Reminiscences of Premyatra: Epilogue.*

Here, please note clearly that *Premyatra* is a scriptural text. Therefore, it must be read repeatedly, contemplated continually, and incorporated into everyday life. Truly, *Premyatra* is a textbook that incorporates many of the personal insights I have discovered and have used effectively.

In addition, I have read the discourse manuscripts, chapter by chapter, to my dear disciple Amrit Desai as a teaching tool. He made important contributions after listening very attentively to each word of every discourse. To commemorate my pilgrimage to America, he and his entire family of disciples have already published the Gujarati version of this text and are very eagerly awaiting this English edition.

This yoga textbook and scripture has a very unique structure that allows for problems to arise. So, at this point, I would like to provide some clarification on an issue you might be wondering about, "Is this text written for only a special class of people?"

No, the honest truth is that this text is not written with any one group in mind. I can say, with no exaggeration, that this textbook is written for everyone in the world, since yoga is indeed the mother of all knowledge. Around the world, in fact, yoga has been validly termed the "knowledge of the Self," "the knowledge of the Supreme Being," and the "path to liberation."

This first volume of *Premyatra* treats the yamas and niyamas in great detail. Although these are only the first two stages of yoga, they condense within themselves the genuine principles of every religion in the world. These yamas and niyamas have been widely proclaimed in the yogic scriptures as disciplines required for every human being, whether he is a worldly person or a renunciate, and regardless of his country, caste, or sect. It is noteworthy that dharma is defined as "anything that fosters development in the individual, family, society, nation, or world," and that this universal dharma requires everyone to follow these great disciplines.

The yamas and niyamas build a person's character so thoroughly that, by sincerely practicing them, one can cease to be an animal and can become transformed into a human being or the Lord. And, yet, although these practices are very arduous, fear is unwarranted, because we are required to practice them only to the best of our capacity. It is said that one can drink only as much water as he can hold, no matter how much water the river holds.

Then, too, these yamas and niyamas are very special in another way. It is definitely worth remembering that the successes achieved by influential men and women in their various fields are all founded upon the practice of these yamas and niyamas. Although some successful people may be unaware of yoga, each of them practices willful disciplines. These practices resemble the yamas and niyamas and foster the development of orderliness, eagerness, patience, courage, and faith. It is a fact that, for whatever reason, every individual's core personality development depends fundamentally upon his practice of these yamas and niyamas. Summarized briefly, I can confidently state that anyone who ignores this spiritual science of yamas and niyamas is clearly stunting his own development.

Psychology is the specialized science of the mind, and behavior and yoga comprise the vast science of the Self. Yoga focuses first on the mind stuff, or chitta, then the organs and prana; and beyond these its focus lies on the soul, where the ocean of knowledge is continuously roaring. Thus, from the viewpoint of yoga, psychology plays a very small role in the spiritual science of yoga but a very large role among the material sciences. Indeed, psychology can be considered the root cause of every material scientist's discovery; because, if each of those scientists had not explored his own mind and behavior, he could have never made his discovery.

The profound meaning of yoga can be understood, in varying degrees, only by those who are interested enough to study it systematically through personal experiments. Anyone interested in yoga should study this textbook carefully and then be sure to contemplate it deeply. Sadhaks must continually study the yogic texts, because these are necessary

keys for opening the door of knowledge and realizing the truth.

For this reason, a sadhak should not become impatient if the segment of society that stays continually busy with worldly duties does not accept this textbook. Instead, he should notice the success of the segment of society that does accept this book, so that he will also become attracted to it.

To date, countless commentaries have been written by various authors expounding the original scriptures of spiritual science. These commentaries have proven useful to all. To beginning sadhaks, they point out the proper path and provide initial inferences helpful to them in drawing personal inferences from everyday life. However, if some sadhaks, as they develop their own inferences begin making changes in the original texts, these changes could spread everywhere and the original texts would not remain intact.

Nothing in this world can ever match, in quality or in quantity, the pure, unadulterated truth. Truth is the ocean of beauty itself. Truth is the source of all the beauties of the entire universe. Not everyone has experienced truth, however; it can be experienced only by the rarest person. Ordinary eyes are unfit for seeing the plain truth, since this always requires a divine eye. Sometimes people will actually try to spread the plain truth by decorating it in various ways with untruth. Yes, everyone falls head over heels for this fancy truth, but they still remain stuck in the same place. Adulterated truth will never move anyone from the darkness of ignorance to the light of truth.

Next to the vastness of truth, the human being is the size of an atom. And if truth is pleased by that atom, it is only by truth's greatness that it may decide to condescend to human level. On the other hand, if human beings want truth to fit them, it is only by their lowliness that they try to cut it down to their size; and they succeed only in making themselves smaller than they already are. Thus, we should never attempt to alter the truth at all; we should alter ourselves instead. Why? Because this is the best way to move from insignificance to greatness and it fits within the natural laws of development.

And yet, of course, it is only natural at first for new students of any subject to consider the terminology of that subject uninteresting. But do not forget that the special language of every science is its only entrance gate. For the traveler to eventually reach the huge courtyard of its knowledge, he must enter the gate of that science and traverse its narrow lanes and alleyways.

The essence of any science is locked in seed form within each of its esoteric terms. We can attain the light of truth in that science only by assimilating that essence. Thus, scientific terminology should be kept in its original form so that the subject to which the terms refer remains more accessible. Yes, it is always possible to replace the original terms with new synonyms, and this will make the subject seem more familiar and interesting; but the changes in meaning would prevent the seeker from reaching the feet of the truth. I believe that in the material sciences, under special circumstances and to a slight extent, such changes may be permissible. But, in yoga science, any alterations are absolutely contraindicated.

Knowledge of the Self is such an abstruse and extremely esoteric science that technical terms are purposely coined which have only a single, specialized meaning. Every seeker must cling to that single true meaning and renounce all other meanings misattributed to it. But not everyone can practice such discrimination, even though yoga sadhana cannot even begin until its secret is truly told. So, the seeker must understand the original meaning of the terminology. To do so he must sit at the feet of a series of experienced masters as a devoted disciple until he receives an adept Sadguru; and, eventually, his critical problems come to an end.

Thus, the seeker must be patient for a long time before he can understand even the theoretical aspects in the scriptures of yoga science; and these must be understood first before he can travel the path of sadhana according to the guidance of an experienced Sadguru.

Yes, to merely attain scriptural knowledge, the sadhak must pursue austerities so arduous that this tapas itself becomes transmuted into profound devotion. Always remember that genuine yoga sadhana cannot ever begin before this profound devotion arises.

I conclude with my heartfelt wish that this text may be helpful to all seekers.

Jai Bhagwan: I bow to the divine within you,

Bapuji: Your loving father,

Kripalu

Muktidham
Kripalu Yoga Ashram
Sumneytown, PA
U.S.A.

Chapter 1

Celibacy

Ancient Yoga Science vs. Modern Psychophysiology	3
Sincerity in Celibacy	6
The Importance of Conserving Sexual Energy	7
The Results of Unrestrained Sexual Activity	8
The Vow of Celibacy: Secret to Growth	8
The Practice of Unconditional Love	9
The Practice of Unrestrained "Free Love"	13
Anecdote: Vasavdatta meets Upgupatta	14

8 July 1977
Friday, 6:15 a.m.
Kripalu Yoga Retreat
Summit Station, PA

My dear children,
All my life I have deeply contemplated the subject of celibacy or brahmacharya. Truly, this is the most important subject for all of mankind. Today, I will present some aspects of this subject to you.

Ancient Yoga Science Vs. Modern Psychophysiology

Our current concept of celibacy is very different from the ancient concept of brahmacharya held by the ascetic sages of India[1]. In comparison, our current understanding and experience of celibacy is superficial. These ancient sages conducted scientific experiments of the highest order on the nature and problems of celibacy. To solve the celibacy problem, they based their experiments on the ancient and highly developed science of yoga. Our present knowledge of celibacy is based on contemporary concepts from biology, physiology, medicine, psychology and philosophy which are derived from very superficial experiments and experiences. Therefore, the two concepts of celibacy differ greatly in meaning.

Although our limited contemporary view of celibacy may indeed be correct, it is clearly not the view of the ancient sages of India. We cannot, therefore, rule out their point of view until we understand celibacy from within the context of their unique experience.

Modern scientists claim that it is not possible to achieve total celibacy; and this viewpoint cannot be totally refuted since it has scientific support. *Both the physical and spiritual sciences are equally valid and significant.* I have contemplated this subject for only fifty years, whereas the ancient sages of India have contemplated it for thousands of years. A thousand years from now the modern geniuses of physical science may

[1] rishi munis

be forgotten. But the adept spiritual scientists of ancient India practiced for thousands of years and have not been nor will ever be forgotten. Their knowledge transcends the limits of body, mind, and intellect and has entered the unapproachable realm of the soul.

Spiritual science is variously termed "knowledge of the Self," "knowledge of yoga," "science of the Self," and the "science of yoga." This holistic science is the treasure house which integrates both the spiritual and the physical sciences. Those who believe that India is the source of spiritual science only are deluded. *However, unless physical science is first developed, spiritual science cannot be attained; because physical science forms the very base of spiritual science.*

In the forests of ancient India, experiments were conducted on various subjects. These experiments were systematically repeated to replicate and validate the obtained results. These spiritual scientific principles are not ordinary; they are extraordinary and eternal.

Modern physiologists claim to have discovered that total celibacy is not possible; but this is not new research. The same research work was performed thousands of years ago. At that time, on the basis of ordinary research, the discovery of this extraordinary research occurred. For example, in chapter three of the *Bhagavad Gita*, passion is demonstrated to be evil, and a technique to overcome it is advanced. Moreover, the spiritual science tradition recognizes the experiences of the guru and Sadguru as valid bases for experimentation, just as the physical science tradition recognizes the empirical results of one's predecessors as a valid starting point for testing his own hypotheses. To believe in the experiences of someone else is one thing, but to evaluate those experiences through one's own personal experimentation is another. The conclusions of the ancient spiritual pioneers were not only based upon logic, but upon systematically collected experimental evidence.

Consider these two hypothetical principles: (1) "Celibacy is possible" and (2) "Celibacy is not possible." Hypothesis two is proposed by physical science and may appear more valid to you, because it is derived from and applied to general society. However, if you want to become a sadhak, you will have to accept hypothesis one, which is based on spiritual science. You will have to analyze why these two views of celibacy are different and to what extent they differ. No technique is needed to test the second hypothesis; but as a spiritual scientist testing the first hypothesis, you will need a technique to uphold and maintain the celibacy necessary to continue experimenting.

The modern psychiatrist, Sigmund Freud, postulated that sensual desire pervades and drives all human beings. However, this is not new research. Ancient Indian yogis also accepted this principle, and it is not necessary to go to great lengths to understand it. *Since birth itself results from the sexual act, it is only natural that passion predominates human life.*

Dr. Freud believed that someone who kisses a baby is essentially motivated by sexual desire. Scientifically, this is partly true. But we need to accept this premise with discrimination. Kissing a baby involves low-level sensual desire. Formally embracing a young child or affectionately tapping a child on the head or body involves medium-level desire. Both these desires should be considered affectionate and distinguished from passion-provoking desire. Rejecting this distinction presumes that the affectionate behavior of father, mother, and guru are necessarily motivated by sensual desire, which is not true. It is incorrect to consider the affectionate speech or touch during ordinary human interaction to be primarily motivated by sexual desire.

If we consider sensual desire to be one pole of a continuum and selfless desire the other pole, it would be unscientific to accept one and reject the other. For example, I am the guru of numerous disciples. When someone comes to me with sadness and tears, they often cry out even from a distance. Wishing only to lighten their heart, they cry in an emotional manner and place their head in my lap or at my feet. Often, I must touch them to console them. At this time, only streams of pure affection are flowing in my mind. Likewise, the infant touches the mother's breast while breastfeeding. It is incorrect to consider this act as being motivated by sensual desire.

Of course, while genuine exceptions may exist, it is desirable for a yogi to refrain from touching women. In India, for example, there are four well-known ashrams of Jagadguru Shankaracharyaji. The spiritual mentors of these ashrams do not allow women to touch their feet. If an unknown woman mistakenly touches them, they fast for the rest of the day. (This does not imply that the woman's touch has defiled them, however; since touching a holy saint's feet with pure feelings is not harmful for anyone.) Moreover, many well-known saints will not be alone with a woman. It is natural for jagadgurus to be considered fathers or gods, and their touch is sacred for all. But at the same time, the discipline of not touching to maintain holy traditions is established for the public welfare and well-being.

Sincerity in Celibacy

After considering all of this, you may consider it impossible to sincerely practice celibacy. The possibility of maintaining a rigorous conscientiousness toward celibacy can be demonstrated, however, through an in-depth analysis of the apparent contradictions. Evidence exists from many celibates that focusing upon the positive benefits of celibacy can cultivate self-confidence, perseverance, courage, and patience. On the other hand, dwelling upon the difficulties and obstacles to celibacy can clearly retard progress.

However, I believe that those who have enjoyed sports and exercise during their formative childhood years have the easiest time sincerely observing celibacy. Through their ongoing awareness of the benefits of celibacy, their thinking process gradually expands and develops, which in turn increases their purity and dedication in the practice of celibacy.

On the other hand, those who have had sensuous lifestyles throughout their formative years become the victims of sensuality and have difficulty cultivating a conscientious attitude toward celibacy. Moreover, even if the need for celibacy awakens, their mental weakness prevents its cultivation. Thus, one's repeated experience of sensuality promotes addictive behavior in addition to the firm belief that he has no choice but to yield to sensual desires. Conversely, one's repeated experience of sexual abstinence promotes the realization that abstinence is possible and that sensuality can actually be overcome.

The Importance of Conserving Sexual Energy

Children and adolescents often appear attractive and strong, since much energy is accumulated during childhood and adolescence. Conversely, middle-aged and elderly people often appear enervated and repulsive because much energy is lost during these stages. Moreover, just as the energy generated by steam or electricity powers machines which perform great tasks, the celibate can also accomplish amazing tasks by conserving sexual energy.

By conserving virya, one can defend the entire universe. One can establish his eminent position in society like the sun

among the moon, planets, and stars. Even the closed doors of fate and fortune are opened by conserving virya. By doing so, one's physical radiance gradually increases. The sadhana of sexual conservation is genuine sadhana; because, through it, one can accomplish whatever he desires. Indeed, he can even be freed from the bondage of birth and death.

The Results of Unrestrained Sexual Activity

When a person indulges in unrestrained sexual activity, he loses his storehouse of life energy. Such activity progressively destroys strength, intellect, patience, and memory. It fills our lives with sorrow, agitation, restlessness, boredom, and depression. Those who do not conserve their sexual energy are rejected wherever they go and meet failure in whatever they do. Just as everyone discards mango peelings and pits, those who waste sexual energy are rejected by everyone. Their bodies become lusterless and riddled with innumerable diseases, and hoards of problems attack them insidiously.

The Vow of Celibacy: Secret to Growth

One need practice sexual abstinence for only one year and one-quarter to experience its pervasive benefits. This is the best method one can use to begin experiencing the benefits of celibacy. Do not forget that passion is an enemy to life, but sensual restraint is a friend. It is foolish to fear a friend, and it is weakness to imagine that you could never observe a vow of celibacy.

You should cast out such evidence of infirmities from your mind and awaken your dormant sense of determination.

Those with mere verbal valor claim to kill big tigers, but they are actually afraid of dogs. They break a morning vow in the afternoon and an afternoon vow in the evening. Some are so weak that even when encouraged with millions of words, they do not act fearlessly. Valor can only be instigated in a valiant person, not a coward. The valiant warrior remains valiant. Even after he is beheaded, his body continues to fight.

Moreover, a vow is like a goddess or a virtuous lady who will marry only a valiant warrior.

Upon taking a vow, you should abandon your former negative environment and sensual friends. Just as the engine of a train provides the energy to pull the cars, an environment suitable for celibacy among friends who practice restraint provides energy for someone with poor self-control. At the start of a vow, you need to clearly understand the importance of celibacy and to firmly establish your dedication to practice. You should then take the vow and begin experimenting with it.

With the systematic practice of yoga, you should erect a fortress of prayer, moderation in diet, exercise, study of holy books, and other necessary disciplines. Prayer refers here to the natural devotion or sentiments generated while in sorrow or joy. Moderation in diet means a balanced diet, eating neither too much nor too little. Exercise aids moderation in diet, and practicing both together produces physical alertness and mental joy.

Celibacy, known as "brahmacharya" or "movement toward the Lord," is the guidance which arises within a genuine spiritual seeker who sincerely practices yoga. Such a practitioner enjoys health, happiness, and knowledge! If these benefits are to be yours, you must become a pilgrim on the path of sadhana. Realize, also, that you are the fragrant flower of your family's garden and that your happiness and prosperity become your family's as well.

The Practice of Unconditional Love

A married couple practicing sexual restraint leads a happy life. When the wife expects the husband home from work, she repeatedly goes to the doorstep and stares into the distance while awaiting his return. She is not motivated by sensual desire, but by pure love. Seeing her husband coming in the distance, a new consciousness pervades her entire being. Their eyes meet each other from a distance, and upon approaching each other, their faces light with smiles. Similarly, when the wife is out, the husband eagerly awaits her arrival. In the absense of forceful physical excitement between them, their love has a sweet serenity. Indeed, their love-drenched minds embrace each other. Their life is not ruled by superficial rituals. Of course, their lifestyle has structure and formality; but those with pure love are able to keep the significance of these external behaviors in perspective.

External behavior is meant only to facilitate interaction. If one overemphasizes formalized external behavior, he develops into an adept actor rather than a genuinely loving person. If we continually give verbal thanks to everyone we see, but keep the bag of our genuine gratitude closed, the flower of love receives no nourishment and can never bloom.

The happiness of husband and wife spreads among their children. Men and women who conserve their sexual energy appear younger even during old age. They are envied among those who waste their sexual energy. Health, happiness, and beauty are produced in those who practice restraint. Indeed, in ancient India people would typically live one hundred years because of the well-established heritage of sexual restraint.

The happiness which can be derived from affection free of sensual desire can never be derived from passionate behavior. A brother becomes so happy seeing his sister, a mother seeing her son, a daughter her father. Yet, they're all men and women. Why isn't sensual desire aroused in them? Because there is a significant difference in the way they perceive their relationship to each other. That is the key.

Sadhaks who seek refuge in this different type of relationship with the opposite sex truly relish the experience of divine love and understand the importance of this distinction in perceiving the opposite sex. If one looks upon an older woman as his mother, a woman close to his age as his sister, and a younger person as his daughter, he can receive the same happiness he receives from his own mother, sister, or daughter. The same is true for women considering men either as father, brother, or son. In addition, when a father gently caresses his daughter's head, a mother pats her son, or a brother and sister share lovingly, their affection and pure love merge. Such holiness is a sight which humbles even matrimonial love. If we can expand this affectionate behavior to everyone and extinguish the influence of sensual desire, we can become a living confirmation of the principle: "vasudheva kutumbakam," "the entire world is truly one family."

Pure affectionate behavior never flourishes while one is attached to sensual pleasures. If you wish to develop pure affectionate behavior, grasp this concept firmly: the practice of celibacy is facilitated only when you change your perceptions toward the opposite sex.

When I left my family to wear the saffron clothes of a sanyasi, I picked up an ascetic's wooden pot and was all alone in this world. I had no relatives or loved ones. Only after becoming a swami did I directly realize that I should live according to the principle that the entire world is one family. In this respect, a sanyasi does not abandon his original family; but, rather, expands it to include the whole world. I was only thirty years old when I was initiated as a renunciate. At that time, my reverend Gurudev instructed me to begin addressing older women as "Mother," those my age as "Sister," and those younger than I as "Daughter." By doing so, throughout the years I have continually witnessed the pure love of a mother, sister, or daughter reflected back to me in the eyes, speech, and behavior of various women. Today, on the threshold of old age, when someone calls me "Bapuji" (dear father), I feel streams of affection flowing from my heart. Indeed, only pure love is such an ocean of holiness.

When practicing energy conservation, it is important to realize that the practice of restrained, pure conduct and of unrestrained, wanton conduct are as different as east and west. Wearing white definitely nourishes celibacy, while wearing attractive colored clothes increases your physical attractiveness. Different types of clothing bring out different types of desires; it is almost as if a distinctly different personality emerges. Thus, those who want to conserve sexual energy wear clothes only for modesty and protection. Renunciates either shave their heads or grow long, matted hair. If they allow their hair to grow long, they make no effort to arrange it attractively. In contrast, sensual young men often trim their hair and moustache in various styles, and sensual young women try to look beautiful by styling their hair attractively. This is juvenile mania. This desire gradually diminishes with age.

You can practice conservation of energy only if your attraction to the opposite sex diminishes or if you consciously prevent sensual desires from being provoked while with the opposite sex. Purity of thought is mental hygiene, and it is the only way to attain happiness and a genuine sense of well-being. Holy thoughts are an essential fortress to protect the celibate from the modern sensual society.

The evolution of pure thoughts is impossible without self-control. The United States is prosperous. Prosperity can be attained only by restraint and discipline, since nonrestraint destroys prosperity. I do not like to travel; but in the little traveling I have done in America, I have observed, for example, that sixty-percent of the cars had only one person sitting in them. In India, however, even a big industrialist's car will contain four or five people; and if there is an extra seat, an acquaintance walking along the road is accommodated. Thus, efficient use of energy conserves prosperity, while misuse of energy destroys prosperity.

In this country, millions of tons of grain and scrapped cars are tossed into the ocean. This is a vast misuse of prosperity. *Youthfulness is analogous to prosperity and can be conserved through restraint and wasted through sensual conduct. Although prosperity dissolves old disturbances, it also creates new ones.* Moreover, youths who abstain from sexual activity resolve various conflicts of growing up; whereas, those who waste their sexual energy create various disturbances.

The senses are a storehouse of energy. Careless sensualists endure pain by misusing this energy, and those who abstain enjoy happiness by properly channeling it. Thus, it can be seen that evil thought is like a heavy rock: whoever holds onto it gets drowned in the endless ocean of birth and death. Conversely, pure thought is like a lifeboat: whoever holds onto it is kept from drowning in the ocean of the world.

Thus, the only way to grow is through the practice of unconditional love, thereby strengthening your relationship within the family and society.

The Practice of Unrestrained "Free Love"

As soon as boys and girls reach puberty, their attention is drawn towards their own and others' youthful energies. They become attracted to the opposite sex and overwhelmed by sexual excitement. They decorate their bodies in various ways, yearning to increase their beauty and attractiveness. They are continually drawn to communicating with the opposite sex.

Sensual desires instigate this behavior which can be termed libidinal, wanton, or unrestrained conduct. In a vicious, downward spiral, their sensual desire increases and gradually goes out of control. The lifestyle of many adolescents encourages this downfall. They listen to love songs, enjoy sensuous films, plays, or books, and engage in lustful conversations. They fail to discriminate between unhealthy foods and foods which promote health and well-being; they indulge in meats, liquor, and "junk foods" which detract from their health and energy. This sensual lifestyle is a slippery downward path.

Since we do not experience sexual passion until puberty, we cannot validly consider sexuality a fully innate instinct. During childhood and pre-puberty, the virya is secreted internally rather than externally. Like the pre-pubescent child, the yogi, after accomplishing sabij samadhi, ceases external secretion and begins internal secretion. This process evolves the yogi into the state where the sexual fluid is totally sublimated.[2]

The virya of a completely celibate yogi, whose sexual fluid is totally sublimated, infuses into his blood. Eventually, his body evolves into a Divine Body[3], totally purified by the

[2] urdhvareta
[3] Divya deha

yogic fire.[4] Even sensual men and women become abstinent at the sight of such a yogi, as illustrated in the following anecdote.

Anecdote: Vasavdatta meets Upgupatta

Vasavdatta was a very beautiful prostitute. She entertained aristocrats at her magnificent residence or sometimes at their palatial homes.

One enchanting full moon night, Vasavdatta was engrossed in beautifying her body. She wore make-up, sensuous clothing, and jewelry. Finally, she adorned her hair with fragrant flowers and sprayed expensive perfume on her sari dress. The house became pervaded with a sweet fragrance.

It was time to leave. In the courtyard, the charioteer stood waiting in his chariot.

Feeling delighted, Vasavdatta seated herself in the chariot and directed the charioteer, "Sumantra, this is a radiant full-moon night. Drive along the lakeshore so we can enjoy its natural beauty."

She was going as a beloved to an appointment made by her lover, and her heart was blooming like a thousand-petaled lotus. Her lover's home was in a secluded spot near the lake. As the chariot moved and they approached the lake, her eyes suddenly came to rest upon a figure on the lakeshore.

There sat a Buddhist monk, Upgupatta, meditating with closed eyes. Radiant with the splendor of celibacy, his body glistened in the moonlight. Vasavdatta had never seen such a beautiful sight. She completely forgot the lover she had originally set out to meet. (Was he then her lover? No, for if he were truly her beloved, she could not have forgotten him in such a flash.) She was a prostitute with innumerable lovers, each with eyes thirsty for beauty and passion. How could pure love reside there?

[4]yogagni

Vasavdatta halted the chariot close to the shore. Quietly alighting, she approached Upgupatta. Her jingling anklets caught his attention, and he opened his eyes. Although he beheld a celestial damsel standing before him, Upgupatta was not influenced by her arrival or by her beauty. Vasavdatta peered into his crystal clear eyes which contained neither passion nor the desire for beauty. Never in her life had she seen such a pure and wholesome gaze.

At that moment, her Indian heritage reflected back to her the thought, "He is a saint. His body and mind are very pure. It is a great sin to look at him with passionate eyes."

Yet, this thought did not remain in her mind for long. Vasavdatta had mastered the art of overwhelming her lovers with passion, but now she found herself completely helpless for the first time. Was the thirst for pure love awakening in her?

While drinking in the nectar of his beauty, Vasavdatta found herself gently praying to him, "Oh Divine One! I have accidentally come upon your feet, and in a mere moment I have become yours. Kindly accept me. I humbly beg for your love."

Hearing her request, neither his eyes nor his speech reflected anger or humiliation. Rather, Upgupatta's eyes were flooded with pure love as he replied, "Divine lady, right now I am meditating; let me continue and tomorrow I will come to your home."

Astonished, she inquired, "You'll come to my home?"

"Of course," he replied.

"Your Holiness, do you know who I am?" Vasavdatta asked timidly.

"No, I do not know who you are."

"I am Vasavdatta, a well-known prostitute in this city."

"Where do you live?" came the unconcerned voice of the saint.

"Near the Devkunj."

"All right, then, that is where I will meet you," he said agreeably.

She continued to gaze at him for some time without batting an eyelash, and finally asked, "Wouldn't you hesitate to come there?"

"Where is there hesitancy in love?" he firmly replied.

The word "love" resounded in her ears like the sweet strumming of a stringed instrument. Her mind was exalted. Longing to hear it again, Vasavdatta exclaimed, "Do you love me?"

With sublime steadiness, the saint replied, "A few moments ago, you yourself begged me for love."

Again, Vasavdatta experienced a tender joy and immediately felt awkward. Excusing herself, she said, "I do not want to distract your meditation. I will await you tomorrow at lunchtime."

With that, Upgupatta immediately closed his eyes and continued meditating. Meanwhile, Vasavdatta seated herself in her chariot and directed the charioteer to take her back home.

Over the past few years, Vasavdatta had been playing the game of love. But today the flame of pure love was enkindled of its own accord in the temple of her heart. No longer an erring prostitute, Vasavdatta had now become a pure adolescent. Mentally she had married her chosen husband. Although she could not imagine how long this marriage would last, she smiled radiantly. *She felt that her few moments of exquisite pure love had far surpassed her years spent in passionate pursuits.*

No woman becomes a prostitute of her own accord. Helplessness makes her a prostitute. The eternal qualities of pure love do not leave her even if she is a prostitute. Rather, this pure love lies dormant and determined in her heart.

The next day was auspicious in every way. Vasavdatta carefully bathed and dressed herself in white clothing. Someone unfamiliar with her would have guessed that she was an ascetic from the forest visiting the city. She and her maidservants began transforming her home, removing expensive sensual material from the dining room and replacing it with only a modest carpet. Next, she went to the kitchen and prepared very simple food. Although Vasavdatta had a treasury of golden servingware, she asked the servants to bring plantain leaves for dishes. *How could man-made utensils compare with the sublime beauty of God's creation?*

Vasavdatta finished all her arrangements and eagerly awaited Upgupatta in the gallery. When he arrived, Vasavdatta affectionately welcomed him and invited him to dine. Neither spoke during the meal. Upgupatta's eyes were very pleased at the sight of her external changes.

After sitting for some time, he finally excused himself, saying he had to leave.

"You're leaving?" she replied with fright.

"Naturally," he stated. "I came only to offer alms of love. My purpose is finished. Now I must leave."

"So this is love?" she inquired insistently.

"Yes," he replied. "Whatever satisfies the body and mind with a mere drop is called love."

"Your Holiness! But I have not received the satisfaction of which you speak," asserted Vasavdatta.

"That is due to your own lack of penance," replied Upgupatta. *"One cannot attain love without penance. Only after penance purifies the body and mind can the drop of love nectar be secreted. If a mere drop of poison can cause death, then a mere drop of nectar can imbue immortality."*

"But Divine One!" she protested. "Not only do I belong to this mortal world, but I am even more impure and unworthy than an ordinary woman. My only desire in this life is that you might touch me once more."

Upgupatta stood motionless. He closed his eyes for a moment and then promised her, "Divine and fair Lady, I assure you that I will come one day to bless you with a touch. Your penance is to wait until that time. I give my solemn promise."

"I have faith in your word and will await you," she submitted humbly.

As Upgupatta left, Vasavdatta collapsed to the floor.

Several years passed. Stricken with the dread disease of syphillis, Vasavdatta began to experience its torment. Her beauty was painfully transformed into ugliness daily as the disease ran its course. At the same time, an epidemic of plague struck the city. Vasavdatta also fell victim to its ravages, and along with others who had become infected, she was cast out of the city into a ditch.

One night, when the full moon spread its light upon her, the unconscious Vasavdatta began coming to her senses. Upon opening her eyes, she experienced great thirst but could not get up. Death was too near. Still, she yearned for a few drops of water to wet her parched throat. Looking around, Vasavdatta saw that there wasn't a living person to be found. Only a few dead bodies lay off in the distance. There was no one to quench the thirst of the woman who used to drink water from a golden cup. Her eyes filled with tears; her only desire was for water and there was nothing she could do!

Suddenly, she heard someone's footsteps. Slowly turning her head in the direction of the sound, Vasavdatta was filled with joy and surprise. Upgupatta was coming. Suddenly, distress ran off into the distance while immense joy came running to her side. Indeed it was he. It was the same body, splendid with the light of celibacy, which she had seen on the lakeshore. Now he was here by her side, just as bright and magnificent as ever. Silently he sat down.

In a barely audible voice Vasavdatta exclaimed, "You did come after all! I am so happy. Now I will die in peace."

As Upgupatta took her head in his lap, Vasavdatta cried out loudly, "No! No! Please don't touch me. My sickness will infect your body!"

Indifferent to her plea, he took her head in his lap and said with utmost love, "Fair Lady! Do not trouble yourself about my body. I promised to give you happiness with my touch. I have come to fulfill my promise."

Vasavdatta's eyes clouded with tears. Innumerable times she had experienced pleasure through the sense of touch; but the happiness of this sensation was beyond comparison. This was the touch of God. Her body, which had once competed with the charm of the moon, was now riddled with syphillis. But here was a new sensation! Where anyone else would have been repulsed, Upgupatta was showering divine love upon her.

As soon as he lifted the vessel of water, she remembered that her throat was parched. She opened her mouth. Experiencing her thirst quenched, Vasavdatta fell into reverie: "Are these drops of water or of love?" The taste was love. As Upgupatta's hand affectionately caressed her head, Vasavdatta was satisfied drinking the nectar of love.

In a few moments, Vasavdatta felt her mind descending into unknown depths. The dark shadow of death was approaching her. Attempting to fold her hands in prayer, she looked up at Upgupatta; and with eyes fading into the darkness she greeted him.

Pray daily to the Lord on a regular basis. Observe celibacy, and seek the company of moderate diet and exercise. Slowly proceed on the pilgrimage of life, carrying the lamp of good conduct in one hand and the lamp of sexual abstinence in the other.

My auspicious blessings to you all.

Chapter 2

Nonviolence

The Importance of Spiritual Disciplines and Practices	23
Nonviolence and Violence	24
Nonviolence and the Family	25
Using Goals in Life	28
Animals, Birds, and Love	29
Anecdote: The slave and the lion	30
Nonviolence and Sadhana	35

17 July 1977
Sunday 3:30 p.m.
Kripalu Yoga Retreat
Summit Station, PA

The Importance of Spiritual Disciplines and Practices

Just as one must clean a cup before one can fill it with milk, a sadhak must adequately purify his body and mind before practicing any form of yoga. Each branch of yoga defines this purification process differently. Karma yoga prescribes the spiritual disciplines and practices called yamas and niyamas; bhakti yoga outlines the practice of various rituals and vows; and jnana yoga encourages the removal of impurities, distractions, and the layers superimposed on the light of the soul.

All the highest religious sects in the world have accepted the yamas and niyamas to a greater or lesser extent. Indeed, any religious sect which does not observe these disciplines and practices at all cannot survive long. The great sage Patanjali has signified five disciplines to be observed: nonviolence, truth, nonstealing, celibacy, and nonattachment. He has advised the proper observation of these basic practices which will benefit the entire world. These universally humanitarian disciplines are of primary importance for traveling both the pravritti and the nivritti paths.

In the beginning of yoga sadhana, the sadhak must erect a fortress of yamas and niyamas to protect his sadhana. If he does not fortify his sadhana in this way, he is continually attacked by obstacles which disturb it. There are two ways to fight a battle: from within the closed fort and on an open battlefield. One is required to struggle and fight no matter what field he is in. The five most powerful enemies of yoga are violence, deceit, stealing, sex, and attachment. They obstruct everyone traveling on the path to the Lord. Conversely, the five most powerful friends of yoga are nonviolence, truth, nonstealing, celibacy, and nonattachment. Their protection and defense enable one's sadhana to succeed.

Violence and Nonviolence

Nonviolence is the first of the five spiritual disciplines. Its primary position signifies its primary importance; it is the very seed of these basic spiritual disciplines. Indeed, when this seed sprouts, truth, nonstealing, celibacy, and nonattachment manifest spontaneously. One potent virtue attracts countless virtues; one potent vice attracts countless vices.

This is precisely why the practice of nonviolence is religion without equal; it is the superb practice of religion for everyone.

Nonviolence is called "ahimsa," which is made up of two Sanskrit terms: "a" meaning "not" and "himsa" meaning "violent." Since the scriptures prescribe the practice of nonviolence, you might wonder: "Is violence a tendency of the entire society or only of sadhaks desiring to travel the spiritual path?"

When one analyzes the question from a gross perspective, one determines that neither are violent. Upon making a subtle analysis, however, one affirms that both are violent. That is, when observed from a superficial point of view, we see that both the seeker and the nonseeker are nonviolent.

How do we come to that conclusion? If you were to ask a family of elephants or deer, "Are lions violent or nonviolent?"

The entire family would exclaim in unison, "Lions are violent!"

Similarly, if you were to ask the lion cubs playing near the father lion, "Are lions violent?"

They would immediately reply, "My father is an idol of love. I have not seen violence in any corner of his heart."

This is how gross vision shows partiality. Since neither the families of the elephant, deer, or lion are aware of each other, each family considers their own opinion to be true. Likewise, one who makes a gross evaluation shows partiality in considering the sadhak and nonsadhak to be nonviolent. However, the subtle evaluation is impartial and sees both the sadhak and the nonsadhak to be violent.

Each person possesses the tendencies toward violence to a greater or lesser extent. That is the reason why the great masters have included nonviolence in the universal vow. The principle justification we use in considering ourselves nonviolent is that we never carry weapons. We say, "We don't even think of weapons nor do we even keep a knife or a pin in our pocket! But those murderers are always armed!"

However, one should not forget that weapons come in two varieties: gross and subtle. Those who do not use gross weapons use subtle weapons such as thoughts and words. Thought is unmanifest or subtle speech, and speech is gross or manifest thought. Thoughts and speech can be like poison or like nectar. *Wounds from gross weapons heal in one or more months; but wounds from subtle weapons, which are poisonous, do not heal for a long time.* The way in which we write or speak can bite the other's heart; so we commit violence whenever we speak bitterly. Sometimes our temperament often resembles a very cruel and violent animal, and so we displease our relatives and loved ones by speaking bitter words. So, it is most essential that we observe nonviolence.

An excellent form of nonviolence is selfless love, and the most extreme form of violence is hatred. When hatred grows in excess, an individual commits assault. It is a delusion to believe that violence is not committed unless hatred builds up.

Another misbelief is that violence is committed only by people who perform actions such as fishing or hunting. Violence can be committed anywhere, even in one's own living room! For example, whenever a husband or wife wound one another with bitter words, they are committing a very vicious form of violence.

Nonviolence and the Family

If you want to live a happy family life, do not let any violence in. No doubt, you imagine that wounds from arrows, swords, or bullets might feel unbearable. However, they are really much more bearable than wounds from words. The mind of someone who's in a rage gets so agitated that his eyes harden, his body trembles, and he acts as if he's no longer a human but a demon. He inflicts this torture on his own relatives and loved ones and then expects them to love him. How could that happen? If a house is burned up by fire, a new house can be built; but if a family is burned up by quarrels, a new family can never be rebuilt.

If you do not wish to attain yoga, devotion, or knowledge, don't! But if you want to live happily in this world, you will have to practice spiritual exercises to soften your eyes, heart, thought, and speech. Both the husband and the wife should practice the exercise of speaking sweetly in front of the mirror when the other is not home. And they should not consider this play-acting, either; it is a form of learning to love.

Actors in a play must follow a script, while students who want to learn must firmly form new impressions through repeated practice. Only love can cultivate tolerance or forbearance, because the very nature of love is tolerance. How can one who has not even learned how to express affection ever show tolerance? Tolerance expresses itself as nonviolence, whereas intolerance manifests itself as violence. If you are not victorious in cultivating affection and tolerance, you will definitely meet failure in every area of this life. Worldly sadhana is the first stage. Those who do not successfully pass through that stage can never be eligible for yoga, devotion, or knowledge.

Apathy is the seed of violence. The number of trees of hatred cultivated in the field of the mind are directly proportional to the number of areas in which one is apathetic. When these trees are nourished, they bear fruit in the form of violence. The birth of such trees and their fruit inevitably signals the start of war.

Violence takes the attitude, "It's you against me to the death."

Violence takes this firm conviction and assaults the other, whereas nonviolence takes a protective attitude and defends the other.

Although we read innumerable holy books and listen to countless religious discourses, we still remain as we were and do not change a bit! Isn't this amazing? How could this happen? There is just one answer for this: we're all thought and no practice. In order to start turning our good thoughts into deeds, we must start to gradually bring the unrestrained mind under control.

The root cause of family conflicts is faultfinding or blaming. Since faultfinding influences thought, speech, and conduct, the faultfinder continually unsteadies his mind whenever he ruminates on negativity. One should cultivate the habit of appreciating virtue. By appreciating virtue, pure love increases and manifests in one's thought, speech, and conduct as well. Virtue-finders inspire relatives or loved ones to stop bad habits by showing respect, goodwill, sweetness and affection rather than disrespect, ill will, bitterness, or hate. In a family it is very essential to integrate thought and practice. To start with, the whole family must sit together and decide that they want to have a loving, happy, and service-oriented environment for their family and that each individual would like to live happily and help every other member of the family live happily as well. *Unless we give happiness to others, we will never attain happiness.*

In the course of daily life together, differences of opinion or conduct might arise, but discrimination should be used to remove the source of such conflicts. One should be vigilant against allowing such superficial differences to cause deeper differences in the heart. As the differences of opinion increase within one member's mind, disagreements among family members increase. The head of the household should see the needs of the family and design and conduct simple experiments to intervene accordingly. Complicated experiments would not be effective in the beginning, because one does not learn new skills the moment he starts a new job. Skills come gradually! Aptitude, enthusiasm, faith, patience, and other virtues play an important part in skill development. Failure is inevitable, too, and one must reaffirm his commitment and continue the struggle toward success.

Using Goals in Life

There are two types of people in this world: those who have ideals and those who don't. Every genius in every field inevitably has some kind of ideal which guides and develops his life. People without an ideal can never patiently and consistently focus on any one aim for long. *They'll struggle to accomplish one aim today and another aim tomorrow.*

Many years ago, I stayed in Halol, the same village where Amrit was born. He was a boy of fifteen or sixteen at the time and used to come to me regularly every day. We loved each other deeply. Whenever he came to me for affection, I used to advise him to be loving and virtuous and to practice celibacy so that he would succeed in life. Amrit would take my advice affectionately, contemplate it deeply, and then struggle to assimilate it into his daily life. Since the idea I gave him totally suited his aptitude, he was able to incorporate it, and even today he is still sincerely practicing the same ideal. For this reason alone, he is living a genuine life here in America and is inspiring his disciples to also live a genuine life.

Be idealistic! *An ideal should not be accepted immediately, but only after considerable contemplation.* If the ideal suits one's personality, even to a slight degree, it will be easier to practice. But if it contradicts one's personality, it becomes more difficult to practice and eventually must be abandoned anyway. One who forgets his ideal is not a sincere person. Just as flowers carry their fragrance and lamps carry their light wherever they go, idealists carry their ideal wherever they go.

Now, I will try to give you brief suggestions to aid your daily practice.

1. Make it a habit to rise early in the morning. Immediately upon awakening, remember the Lord if only for two minutes. Then quietly finish your regular morning bathroom routine and repeat the name of the Lord or chant a bhajan or dhun.
2. After freeing yourself from your morning routine, meditate in a private place. If you fill your sadhana room full of pure and holy thoughts, it will always bring you to steadiness immediately upon entering it. In this way you should make

your sadhana room a temple of God, a place of pilgrimage, and a land of austerities for you.

3. During sadhana, seek refuge in postures, pranayam and other yoga practices to purify the body. To purify the mind, seek the support of prayers, mantra chanting, bhajan, meditation, reading holy scriptures, and other practices of knowledge. Perform all your actions lovingly rather than mechanically. In this way, you will integrate the approaches of action, devotion, and knowledge to excel in life.

4. Perform group prayers both in morning and evening. Every day after prayer, inspire everyone to behave lovingly. Accept each other's faults and beg forgiveness from one another for your faults.

If a furious lion can be tamed by love, why can't our own relatives, who are not so violent, be controlled? To study the mantra of love is as good as studying the mantra of nonviolence. There is no place for violence in love. Love means self-surrender.

Animals, Birds, and Love

Love also has an influence on animals and birds. While on my way to the chapel here from my residence today, the ashram cat had caught a mouse in his mouth and was walking toward the ashram. Right after witnessing an act of violence, I am seated here before you to teach about nonviolence.

Perhaps after finishing his lunch he may come here to the chapel, before even washing his mouth, and sit in the lap of any one of you. If he actually did so, we could say that one who has acted violently just a moment before is now playing lovingly with you. The feelings which were there in his mind while catching the mouse do not exist while sitting in your lap.

Then, doesn't the cat know how to love the mouse? Yes. Cats always love mice. It does not matter if the cat has never set eyes upon the mouse before! And no matter how sad he may be, he will immediately become happy at the sight of any unfamiliar mouse. But a mouse can never love any cat no matter how joyous the cat may feel. The moment a mouse sees a cat, he becomes immediately dejected. A mouse could never love a cat, and a cat could never hate a mouse. This is Nature's Law or the Lord's Play.

We love birds and animals. And birds and animals can feel our love and love us in return. If even a mouse-killing cat routinely succumbs to our love, why wouldn't our father, mother, brother, sister, son, daughter, wife, and the rest of our family invariably succumb to our love? Wouldn't they at least have the discretion of a killer-cat?

Anecdote: The slave and the lion

Today I'll tell you a story which goes back to the age of slavery in a particular—but unnamed—country.

Once upon a time, there was a slave who desperately wanted to escape the tortures inflicted by his master. One dark night he seized his chance to run from his master's house. When he eventually came to the edge of a large forest, he was tired by his long run and decided to rest there beneath a large tree. He thought to himself, "Well, the forest seems to be a safer haven than the city."

So, feeling safe, rested, and pleased with himself, he entered the forest.

He had now been walking for three days and eating only whatever wild fruit he could find along the way. Until now, food had been only a minor problem, since his major concern had been attaining freedom. Now his desire for freedom was fulfilled.

But the slave did not know that he had chosen a part of the forest that was inhabited by large, ferocious beasts until he suddenly heard the roar of a lion. His body began to tremble uncontrollably, and his heart raced wildly with fright.

Turning his eyes skyward, he began praying fervently, "Oh Compassionate One! I have struggled hard to free myself from slavery. I have not had even a moment to enjoy my freedom before being faced with the threat of immediate death. If you desire my death now, however, I am prepared to come to you."

The lion roared again, and the slave looked all around. Even more fear flared up when he spotted the lion sitting nearby under a large tree. But, curiously enough, the lion did not seem to be interested in him. The expression on the lion's face even seemed to show some pain. The slave began to realize that, after all, the lion's roar had not been the roar of the hunt, but a cry of pain. When this dawned on the slave, his fear began to subside.

It seemed that both the lion and the slave were unhappy. They were two individuals in distress whose paths had crossed by chance. Under these circumstances, it is easy for one who is suffering to have sympathy for a fellow-sufferer.

The slave stood up and approached the lion. He saw that one of the lion's hind legs was so infected by a thorn that he could not get up. Yes, the lion had been roaring from the pain of his wound.

The slave felt great sympathy at the sight of the lion's pain. Compassion is so incredible! Imagine, a bond of tender feelings between a human being and a wild lion!

The slave sat beside the lion and looked at the wound. He saw a very large thorn deeply embedded in the lion's leg, and, after gently extracting it, he tossed it into the underbrush. Next he found a small stream nearby, and, fashioning a makeshift cup from some leaves, he filled it with water. He gently pressed the wound to squeeze out the pus, and then cleaned it with water. Fortunately, the slave had some knowledge of medicinal herbs. After briefly foraging the forest floor, he found a choice herb which he picked and pounded to a pulp. With this salve, he gently dressed the lion's wound.

The lion was obviously pleased by the slave's tenderness and care. He had sensed from the beginning that this newcomer to the forest was a friend, not an enemy.

During the next two days, the lion and the slave became close friends. The lion could walk with some effort by then, so the slave would lead his limping friend to the stream for a drink. Although the lion had been hungry for three days, his love for the slave had so occupied his mind that he didn't notice his hunger.

In a few days the wound was healed. The lion could now hunt freely in the woods. Each day the lion would return from his hunt to sit beside his friend. Wordlessly and with great affection, the two would sit together and gaze into each other's eyes.

Then one day, after about a month of close companionship, the slave decided to try his luck in the city; and the companions parted company reluctantly. As the slave walked away, he looked back at least a dozen times to glimpse his new-found friend sitting at the edge of the forest watching him leave.

The slave entered the city.

In those days any slave without a master was fair game for whoever wanted to possess him. A rich man noticed the slave loitering about and caught him. Fortunately for the slave, however, this new master was a loving man, not mean and cruel like his former master. He was immediately grateful for the kind way his new master treated him, so he began serving his master with love and soon became his favorite slave.

One day his new master heard of a fabulous prize offered to whoever would dare to wrestle with some ferocious lion that had just been captured in the nearby forest. He decided to attend the spectacle. Back then it was a popular entertainment to watch trained wrestlers try to fight fierce animals which had been captured in the forest.

On the day of the event, a large crowd gathered in the arena, including the master and his slave. Everyone was excited because famous wrestlers from all over the kingdom had come to compete for the prize money. Those who had arranged the match had not allowed the wrestlers to see the lion beforehand, however, and as soon as the ferocious lion was displayed, all the wrestlers refused to compete!

The spectators felt disappointed because it seemed that there was no one brave enough to wrestle the lion. The now desperate sponsors offered "the prize of his choice" to anyone who would wrestle the lion. But still no one came forward.

Suddenly, the slave's eye fell upon the cage of the lion. With a start, he realized that it was his friend pacing in the

cage. He said to his owner, "Master, I would like to try for the prize, but under two conditions: first, that I be able to love the lion, not wrestle with him, and second, that I be given the lion itself as my reward."

The master was startled by the slave's strange request, and yet he could see the slave's earnestness. Something in his slave's manner convinced him to go approach the sponsors of the event. The sponsors were surprised, but they consented to the slave's conditions.

Addressing the departing crowd, the sponsors announced, "Brothers and Sisters! Although there is not a wrestler in the house courageous enough to fight this fierce lion, one slave has come forward and has volunteered to try and love him!"

Many spectators laughed; others were concerned or even worried for the slave; and all began to discuss the meaning of this turn of events. When the slave stood up and approached the cage, some speculated that he was so fed up with his life that he decided to end it with a daredevil stunt.

As the slave approached the cage, the crowd burst into spontaneous applause and cheers. Everyone felt their heart skip a beat as he opened the cage door. They were convinced that as soon as he stepped into the cage, the lion would pounce on him and kill him.

When he was first brought into the arena, the lion had roared so loudly that several children in the audience fainted. How could such a fierce lion welcome the love of a slave?

As the slave opened the cage door, his eyes met those of the lion. The old friends were delighted to see each other again! The slave entered and gently hugged the lion around the neck while the lion affectionately licked his friend's face. The audience was dumbstruck, then enchanted, as if a spell had been cast upon them! No one could fathom this turn of events. Was this a slave or a magician?

Yes, this was truly magic taking place before their very eyes; the magic of love. For if there is one thing in this world which is truly magical, it is love.

The arena was near a small hill outside the city walls. A pathway just beyond the hill led directly to the forest. The slave had decided beforehand to set the lion free, and the sponsors had agreed to his conditions.

Their bond of love was over.

Coming to the door of the cage, the slave addressed the crowd, "My respected elders, please give me your attention. Do not be afraid. My friend and I will now quietly and peacefully walk to the forest. I wish to see him safely home. Six months ago, the hind leg of this lion was infected by a thorn wound. I happened to be in the forest at that time and came upon him. Seeing his pain, I helped heal his wound and we have been best friends ever since. I am not a magician. What I have done did not come from magic, but from love."

This explanation satisfied the crowd.

The slave reentered the cage and emerged with the lion; but despite his assurances, the crowd was still fearful. The lion was so entranced by his savior, however, that it paid no attention to the crowd. Within a few moments, the two friends disappeared behind the hill as the crowd looked on in astonished disbelief.

Nonviolence and Sadhana

Stability of the mind is essential in sadhana. Nonviolence in sadhana is observed according to the kind of sadhana practiced, and nonviolence in the family is observed according to one's family situation. Ashramites should consider the ashram residents as their family and behave lovingly.

When one practices ahimsa, or nonviolence, one refrains from causing distress—in thought, word, or deed—to any living creature.

Ripples are produced by sand particles, a pebble, or a stone falling into the steady water of a lake. Similarly, unsteadiness arises due to birth of any mutation in the mind. Violence is mutation, or abnormality; and non-violence is nature, or normality.

There are three standard stages of sadhana—ordinary, medium, and best. Similarly, there are three standards of nonviolence—ordinary, medium, and best. An ordinary sadhak can't practice either the medium or best variety of nonviolence because he lacks the capacity. He has to increase his capacity gradually.

One's mind becomes unsteady when he feels hatred towards someone. If in this situation one enters the meditation room and meditates, it is only natural that thoughts of hatred will capture his mind. As a result, hatred will be rooted more firmly. The sadhak has to remove the hatred, and, in such situations where he can't, he should never enter his meditation room. Those who meditate do so in a place where they are more comfortable. It can also be said that a place where an individual can continually repeat a single thought is his meditation room, whether it's a bedroom or a lavatory. Those people who steal, cohabit, or assault will engage in similar evil actions. Vicious and virtuous actions alike are merely the results of concentration.

Whenever the sadhak's mind becomes unsteady due to any abnormal thought, he should make it steady by engrossing himself in some activity which he likes or for which he has an aptitude. The situation which increases the unsteadiness of the mind should be firmly abandoned. Only the sadhak who has accomplished the art of changing the direction of the mind can become a master. Unsteadiness of the mind is an obstacle. An undesirable obstacle can only be removed by a desirable obstacle. Only a thorn can pluck out a thorn. It is worth remembering here that one should not lift a sword against another sword; instead, one should raise a shield against a sword. One has a right to defend the blow, but not a right to initiate the blow. This technique is for the sadhak on pravritti path, not for the sadhak on the nivritti path.

Here some explanation is necessary. A traveler on the pravritti path is devoted to virtuous conduct and thoughts and is always vigilant. However, when the dependent prana in his body becomes independent, his steady, strong mind becomes unsteady and weak. In the beginning, the sadhak repeatedly experiences failure in such situations, and his firm mind becomes excited because of repeated failures. However, if he determines under what circumstances the dependent prana becomes independent and then he erects obstacles to its independence, he is able to resist failure.

Suppose someone abuses a sadhak. If he does not tolerate it, then the bodily dependent, controlled prana becomes free and disturbs the mind. As a result, the sadhak may abuse someone to counteract abuse or even commit an assault out of anger. This is the state of affairs while one is wide awake. If the same situation arises during the state of sleep, it will also have the same result. Therefore, a sadhak on the pravritti path has to have a subconscious mind with the same impressions of the conscious mind. Only then can the disturbances of the dream be restrained.

Although this single illustration is enough, I will give you another. When one sees a picture of a beautiful woman, the dependent, restrained prana becomes independent and disturbs the mind. In this situation, too, one has to make an attempt to lead the mind in the opposite direction. This is known as resistance. Since such a disturbance can also arise in the dream state, the sadhak has to make his subconscious mind devoted and dutiful too. Thus, some changes or variations are born due to susceptibility to physical or external disturbances, whereas others are due to susceptibility to mental or internal disturbances.

On the pravritti path, external and internal stability indicate predominance of the mind, whereas instability indicates the predominance of prana.

When a sadhak on the nivritti path is engrossed in the meditation of surrender to prana in his sadhana room, then the thoughts of attachment and hatred are born spontaneously.

A traveler on the pravritti path restrains the prana while strengthening his mind. During his meditation, he does not allow disturbances to rise in his mind. If such a disturbing thought rises, the mind curbs the prana and renders it helpless. The traveler on the nivritti path, on the other hand, restrains his mind while strengthening the prana. During his meditation, prana awakens even the latent mental passions and fights them too. However, it can't overcome them; it meets repeated failure. Despite this fact, it does not abandon fighting. Eventually, it becomes very strong and attains victory over them.

Here, too, a little explanation is necessary. On the pravritti path more mental passions are produced, and on the nivritti path more physical passions are produced. It can also be stated that external excitements function in the pravritti path, and internal excitements function in the nivritti path. A sadhak on the pravritti path is cautious against allowing passions to rise. He obstructs them and prevents their disturbing his mind. A sadhak on the nivritti path, however, while in meditation does not obstruct the passions. Instead, he deliberately awakens them and tolerates the disturbances of mind caused by them. In the beginning, due to past impressions, the sadhak likes many of these passions.

However, when prana continually awakens those same passions, then, because of their abundance, the sadhak's attachments are gradually weakened. This is the middle stage.

In the beginning stage prana continually awakens the same passions which cause the arousal of malice in the sadhak's mind. Eventually, however, he becomes indifferent. In this way, the sadhak of sahaj yoga, triumphs over the mind through prana and attains liberation.

If the nivritti dharma sadhak associates himself with any activity, seeks the company of many people, becomes more talkative, and observes disciplines indiscriminately, distractions arise in his sadhana. In order that distractions do not arise, he should observe seclusion, silence, and abandon the company of people and such other unfavorable activities. Yes, he should behave affectionately with others. However, by secluding and abandoning the company of people, he can observe nonviolence more easily.

Chapter 3

Truth

The Meaning of Truth	41
Truth and the Family	41
Silence: The First Step Toward Truth	42
Anecdote: The businessman of Bengalgranus and seclusion	45
Discrimination in Speech: The Second Step Toward Truth	48
Anecdote: Do not answer this notice!	49
Disciplined Speech	50
Anecdote. A sweet joke	50

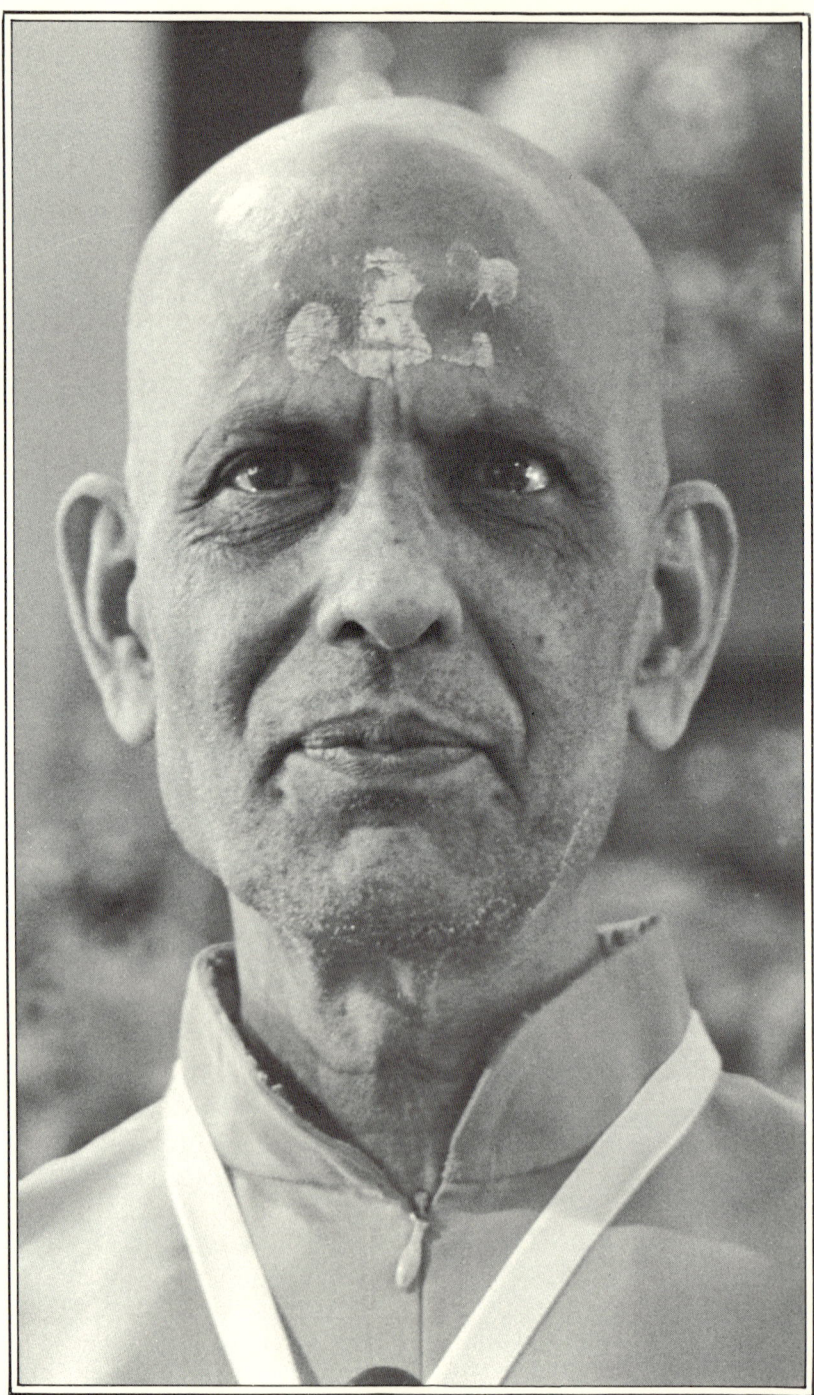

19 July 1977
Tuesday
Kripalu Yoga Retreat
Summit Station, PA

The Meaning of Truth

Today I will present to you some important aspects of the second yama, or spiritual discipline, called "satya" or "truth." Among the countless possible meanings of truth, I have selected the meaning of "truth in speech" to discuss today. Truth is defined as "that which promotes the welfare of all living beings and which is not adulterated with untruth." Spiritual masters who have realized the truth and who have lived their lives according to this definition eventually feel that the whole world is their family. Since these saints have dropped all ego and become free, their every action is, consequently, inspired by the Lord, nature, or the social welfare. People who are so totally free have no reason to speak less than the full truth. Please remember, however, that this stage culminates a very long period of practicing truth in speech.

Truth and the Family

Great masters who have realized the ultimate truth actually come to us carrying a brilliant lamp which disperses the darkness of untruth. Just as an owl can't tolerate the light of day, we can't tolerate the light of truth; so we hide the truth behind our backs and live in the farthest corner of the untruth. The word truth is ancient and has been defined in our dictionaries for hundreds of years; but being staunch devotees of novelty, we refuse to use the word. From earliest childhood, we have developed the habit of speaking untruth. *Our condition is such that we need not worry about practicing truth in speech but merely need to delete a little untruth from the mass of untruth we usually speak. Thus, to practice truth, we should decrease our practice of untruth.*

We cannot have harmony in our family life, because we and our family members do not know how to speak truthfully with one another. Why do we find it so hard to speak truthfully with five to ten relatives and loved ones? If we can't speak truthfully with them, how can we speak truthfully in our larger social systems and the whole nation? We are so devoid of love and so full of selfishness that all we can utter is untruth.

Of course, we all know how to talk well enough, but whether we can call what we say communication is another question altogether. *We cannot truthfully say that we know how to speak simply because we know how to pronounce vowels and consonants. Unless we speak truthfully, speech is only noise.*

A person who speaks truthfully should be considered more than merely courageous; he is supremely valiant. On the other hand, the make-believe valor of one who speaks untruthfully is sheer deception; what seems to be courage is pure helplessness. Untruth erects walls between hearts and turns even loved ones into strangers and enemies. Truth destroys the walls between hearts and transforms even strangers and enemies into loved ones.

Untruth breeds chaos and hatred, while truth breeds love and peace.

Silence: The First Step Toward Truth

Truth is feared by everyone more than anything else in the world, even though it breeds peace and prosperity. Why do we fear truth, which is a form of God and love? We are afraid of speaking the truth for many reasons. One important reason is that we believe that truth is as worthless as a counterfeit coin and cannot help us get what we want in the world. We believe that we must speak untruth in order to get along in life and be happy. Our firm belief that untruth is universally valuable leads us down the primrose path to decline.

Let's say that truth is on the hundredth step. To reach truth, then, we would have to start on step one and walk one-by-one up the ninety-nine steps toward truth. To do this, we need the help of various techniques. A person who needs to catch a snake must start by grasping its vital point with forceps to prevent it from biting him. Although truth is a pot of nectar rather than a poisonous snake, our egotistical traits such as hatred and selfishness are like poisonous snakes. We can only begin to curb our speech and conduct by grasping their vital points with the forceps of silence.

Silence is the first step toward obtaining truth since it helps us curb untruth which we generally express by talking excessively all day. This incessant flood of speech makes us prone to the bad habit of speaking untruth. Now, this habit might be tolerable if it died with our bodies, but it goes on affecting us life after life. Speaking untruth is, consequently, a major cause of our downfall.

The best way to remove the bad habit of speaking untruth is to stay in seclusion. Start by staying one hour, then two hours, then three hours, and gradually increasing the duration of the silence until, eventually, you are observing silence all day on any day that is convenient. You can't count the silence which everyone observes during sleep, however. Count only the time you are deliberately restraining your speech during the waking state.

The most useful way to observe silence is to stay in seclusion. Restraining speech is natural, then, since there's no one around. Anyone who tries to begin observing silence without seeking refuge in this useful technique must tolerate countless disturbances.

But remember: although you restrain your speech when you practice silence, your potent thoughts do not need to be expressed through speech. Silent behavior easily expresses potent thoughts. For example, once someone who was observing silence was abused by someone. All of a sudden, without uttering a single word, he slapped the offender. *The purpose of observing silence is not merely to restrain speech, but to restrain the mind. Just as pulling one end of the carpet draws the whole carpet, restraining one desire controls the entire mind.*

Therefore, in order to accomplish the purpose of restraining speech, one must restrain his behavior. *Just as water can't be stored in a container which has a hole, thoughts can't be controlled in silence in which one exhibits indiscriminate behavior.*

Silence with discrimination is like a wish-fulfilling tree or a touchstone; it has the power to transform an ordinary seeker into an accomplished master. I have observed constant silence for nineteen years. Although I have not noted specifically what silence has given me, it has brought me everything worth having without my asking for it. Silence has enabled me to practice yoga sadhana steadily.

Silence has blessed me with the habit of practicing self-observation. Silence has constantly kept me awake and aware. Whenever I engage in behavior which I consider improper, my mind is afflicted with great pain. If I cannot spot a mistake in my behavior right away, that very mistake stands before me when I practice self-observation, and I am extremely surprised! If such subtle mistakes spring to my awareness so effortlessly during self-observation, it can only be due to the Lord's grace.

Thought, which is the first stage of the speech process, is subtle, covert, and unverbalized speech. That which we call speech is the overt, gross, verbalized thought which is in spoken or written form and is the second stage of the speech process. One cannot restrain his thoughts merely by restraining speech. On the contrary. When one observes silence and seclusion, even more thought flows are generated. It is as if the mind speaks on behalf of the tongue and then listens to itself on behalf of the ears. Likewise, when one practices meditation, more thoughts arise. Usually, when the seeker performs external activities, his mind is so absorbed in the external environment that he does not realize all the thoughts that are filling his mind. However, when he either observes silence in seclusion or sits for meditation, he becomes introspective. He then becomes acutely aware of the types of thoughts which fill his mind.

Thus, the more a seeker practices silence, seclusion, and meditation, the more introspective he becomes. And, with more practice, he progresses naturally from introspection to self-observation. Only self-observation enables a sadhak to clearly visualize his virtues and vices; and as he progresses in internal purification, his affinity for virtues increases and his affinity for vices decreases.

The seeker who cannot see his true self in the reflection of self-observation cannot become a true sadhak. One who becomes an ocean of virtues through sadhana is truly an accomplished, great master.

Every night, before you sleep, practice self-observation and, then, end your session with prayers.

Anecdote: The businessman of Bengalgranus and seclusion

Silence teaches a seeker to discriminate and contemplate, while talking teaches him indiscretion and unsteadiness.

Once upon a time, a poor orphan boy named Mohan lived in a city among a colony of poor people. Since Mohan's parents had died when he was just a little boy, he was raised by all his neighbors, who pitied him. Now Mohan was no longer a child; he was a young man and could support himself well as a laborer. Everyone loved Mohan because he was naturally loving, generous, polite, tolerant, honest, and quiet-spoken. He had saved some of his wages as a laborer and with it opened up a small shop in which he sold roasted chick-peas. Within a short time, Mohan's honesty caused him to rise from a laborer into a small, highly prosperous businessman.

After becoming prosperous, Mohan got married and eventually had three children. Every Sunday a market was arranged in his section of the city. He would sit there with heaps of bags containing roasted chick-peas and always made a good profit. One Sunday he was going to the market with his cart loaded with bags of chick-peas. He passed other markets on the way which were very crowded. To avoid accidents he would drive his cart very slowly and continually shout, "Hey brother! Please let me by. Oh sister! Please make way for me. Old mother! Please allow me to pass."

At one intersection, the crowd was terribly dense. He continued onward, still shouting, when, suddenly, a child ran right in front of him and was crushed to death under his cart! People gathered around. The police came and recorded an account of the accident.

Mohan's mind was terribly upset. Although he was innocent, he had become very frightened by this misfortune. He made his report to the court, and a day was fixed for his trial.

Today Mohan sat at the Sunday market with his heaps of chick-pea bags and with a very unsteady mind. Tomorrow he must stand trial. His face was full of dark lines of grief. He continually struggled to remove the unsteadiness by praying to God. Suddenly, a sanyasi appeared; he often came to market and would always lovingly receive alms or roasted chick-peas from Mohan.

The renunciate was free of worldly desires, and Mohan and the people of the city loved him dearly. After accepting the alms, he gazed at Mohan's sad face and asked, "Brother, why do you seem so sad today?"

Tears began flowing from Mohan's eyes. After a few moments he became steady and began to relate the story of

his cart accident, concluding with the news that he must stand trial the next day.

Mohan answered a few questions about the accident from the sanyasi who then became contemplative for a time. Finally, he asked Mohan, "During the trial, will you behave as I advise?"

Mohan replied, "I trust you as I do my father and mother."

"Okay," replied the renunciate. "Then, tomorrow when the prosecuting attorney interrogates you, observe silence and continually reflect upon the Lord."

"I will follow your instructions," replied Mohan humbly.

The sanyasi blessed him and then departed.

The next day Mohan went to court. First, the woman whose child had died under the cart recounted the whole incident. Her advocate then began to interrogate Mohan, who remained silent and would not answer a single question. Unable to tolerate Mohan's silence, the woman lost her temper. Interrupting her attorney, she loudly snapped, "Boy! When you were on your way to the market in your cart, your voice was certainly loud enough! You could have broken someone's eardrums shouting 'Make way! Make Way.' Why are you playing dumb now? Why won't you speak?"

Mohan's advocate immediately picked up on this point. Jumping to his feet, he asked her, "When Mohan was shouting so loudly for the right-of-way, while passing through the crowd, why didn't you hold your son? Why didn't you stop him from running?"

The mother could not reply.

After hearing all the testimony, the judge declared Mohan innocent and set him free. Afterwards, Mohan's attorney asked him privately, "Why did you observe silence?"

Mohan replied, "A renunciate living in our city had advised me to observe silence and reflect upon God when the prosecuting attorney interrogated me."

The advocate laughed and said, "Mohanbhai, you may not know it, but that renunciate used to be a famous lawyer before taking the vow of sanyas. Since you were innocent, you were bound to be acquitted; but his advice helped you very clearly demonstrate your innocence."

Although Mohan had observed silence for mere moments, they were just the right moments to stay quiet, so he derived maximum benefits.

Conversely, although the irate mother had let her tongue loose for just a few moments, those were just the wrong moments to let it loose, so she was bound to lose. Silence is a tremendously powerful weapon with surprising protective power.

Observing silence removes many miseries which we gather by gabbing too much. When gentle people speak, it seems like a bottle of perfume has opened. But when boisterous people speak, it seems like a foul-smelling sewer has opened.

Discrimination in Speech: The Second Step To Truth

The second step toward silence and truth in speech is discrimination in speech. A person who habitually talks too much can be firm in observing total silence, but he does not know how to be discreet when he allows himself to speak. It is more difficult to speak discreetly than to keep totally silent, because silence doesn't require the effort of restraint that speaking does. Thus, discrimination in speech is considered to be the step after learning complete silence.

Anyone who is skillful in any action and has achieved financial success as a result of successful verbal communication knows how to observe silence and talk discreetly. *One who places no value on his own speech and misuses it can never achieve success.*

Many people, even lawyers themselves, believe that whoever wants to be a successful lawyer must be eloquent; but this is a mistaken belief. A lawyer must often curb his eloquence and practice discrimination in speech. One who does not know how to use his speech properly can never become a successful lawyer. *A single word from a disciplined speaker is worth more than any number of gold coins.*

Orators read many books, so when they stand up to speak, a cyclone surges from their mouth and shakes the heads of the audience forcefully back and forth. Great masters do not deliver discourses because these require a lot of speaking. How can the audience practice all that is said? Why should a patient suffering from one disease gulp down medicines meant for countless other diseases. Great masters do not show off knowledge; they are like the ancient physicians of India. They give a small packet of knowledge when it is asked for.

Anecdote: Do not answer this notice!

Highly qualified lawyers earn hundreds of thousands of rupees by giving merely a word of advice. They value each word and won't utter a single word that is unnecessary.

I will now narrate an incident related to me by Shri Vitthalbhai Patel, elder brother of Shri Sardar Patel who was an executive for a large corporation. Vitthalbhai received a notice which presented an issue which could cost him hundreds of thousands of rupees.

Although he was a lawyer himself, he felt that he should consult an expert to prevent the organization from suffering a great loss. He went to an expert lawyer and briefly described the entire incident to him. The lawyer replied, "Vitthalbhai, the fee for this advice is 100,000 rupees. Vitthalbhai consented, and the lawyer advised him, "Do not answer this notice."

The lawyer had charged 100,000 rupees for a statement containing twenty letters! However, Vitthalbhai acted according to the advice, and the organization did not suffer a loss.

Disciplined Speech

Lord Shri Krishnachandra preaches that before the spiritual seeker speaks, he must observe several vows: (1) He will always speak only those words which please others; (2) Before uttering a statement, he will first examine every single word to determine if there is any bitterness or selfishness in it; (3) Whatever he says will be for the welfare of others; (4) He will never disturb anyone's mind with his speech; and (5) His statements will be full of truth.

Anecdote: A sweet joke

I will tell you about an incident from my previous stage of life. I was a poet as well as the assistant director of a drama company.

Our drama company was traveling through Kathiawad[1]. To make people laugh, we had an expert comic actor who had performed as the chief comic actor with two famous drama companies of Gujarat. Lately he had been working as a jester with a man from Nawab. After the merger of the states he joined the drama company once again. He had a reasonable grasp of languages such as Gujarati, Hindi, Urdu, Arabic and Farsi. He also understood a little English and Sanskrit. Since we were literary people, whenever we met, we would crack literary jokes. My actor friend was always smiling, and his conduct showed the discretion of a gentleman. Anything he

[1] a province in Gujarat, India, now known as Saurashtra

said or did was civil and would make the audience laugh. In short, he was a skillful and popular actor.

Not only was he a comedian, but he was a deep thinker as well. This unique combination of qualities touched my heart. Although my friend loved both literature and humor very much, he was fully satisfied just being an actor. In spite of having tremendous potential to become a literary scholar, he was unable to progress in that field. Whenever he would seriously discuss this major sorrow in his life, no one observing him could imagine that he was a comedian.

One day I was feeling uncomfortable. My mind would not concentrate on any task. I was pleased when my actor friend arrived unexpectedly. As I sat on a chair on the porch of my residence, he came and sat in front of me on one of the spare chairs. As he began discussing various types of humor in his comical style, I was enchanted and listened wholeheartedly. I soon forgot my unsteadiness. While he was discussing an incident in which he had pulled off a sweet stunt, I saw a brother coming from a distance. This brother was the best actor of the drama company. He was wearing clean white clothes and had very black skin, so his appearance was very bright. I said to the comedian brother, "Friend! Please play a sweet joke on the brother approaching us."

He nodded his consent. Soon the brother approached us and we all greeted one another. Then the comedian said, "Welcome! Welcome!". Then he began to compliment the brother's dazzling white clothes. "Really, it is impossible to resist appreciating your clothes. They are so clean and white that if you were walking on a dark night it would appear as if the clothes were walking by themselves."

I immediately understood the humor in his sweet joke. The comedian had complimented the actor's clothes while criticizing his black skin. He really meant to say, "You are so black that in the dark if there were not clothes on your body it would be impossible to spot you." I was amused by his humor. He was so innocent that he had made a sweet joke that was free of contempt. To prevent the actor from feeling displeased, he had said a second sentence which concealed the satire in the first one.

Thought and conduct are one's life, and speech is one's soul. For this reason, householders and renunciates alike should speak with discrimination. Others like to hear sweet words and hate bitter words just as we do. We should remember this and try to speak so very gently. We should remain vigilant so that we do not mix bitterness and untruth in our speech.

Advice similar to that given in the *Gita* is depicted in Manusmriti [2]. Always remember: "One should speak the truth; one should speak sweetly; one should not speak bitter truth; nor should one speak sweet untruth either. This is sanatan dharma, the eternal truth."

Chapter 4

Nonstealing

The Meaning of Nonstealing	55
Even Saints are Thieves	56
Anecdote: The angel and the hyena	56
Anecdote: The theft of a cloth	58
Yogic Secrets are Kept for the Protection of Yoga, Not for Stealing	62
Anecdote: Dala Tarvadi	64

22 July 1977   55
Friday
Kripalu Yoga Retreat
Summit Station, PA

The Meaning of Nonstealing

Sadhana requires preparation—whether it be yoga sadhana or bhoga sadhana; otherwise, the difficulties one encounters cannot be overcome. It is not easy to perform a task while overcoming obstacles at the same time. For this reason, the best seekers prepare for sadhana by surveying the potential obstacles and erecting a line of defense against them to prevent unexpected difficulties from arising. *Preparation forms the foundation for any task.*

Since we perform all work through the medium of the mind, mental peace and steadiness are essential to the accomplishment of every task. A task is only as easy as the mind is steady, and the body works only as efficiently as the mind is peaceful. *Success in any field of one's choice is possible only when one attains peace of mind.* Thus, before beginning any task, we must prepare ourselves thoroughly by laying a firm foundation. Many difficulties will arise later if we do not realize the importance of this foundation and construct it properly before beginning.

A yoga sadhak is born with a love for yoga, so his primary goal in life is to attain peace of mind. *Only that seeker who squarely confronts the mind's disturbances can practice yoga sadhana.*

We should learn to tackle only one task at a time. So the sadhak should not need to concern himself with external purification when he is purifying himself internally; and when he is purifying externally, he should not need to be concerned with internal purification. Only when the thought stream flows in a single direction does the sadhak achieve quick success.

Nonstealing is the fifth discipline prescribed and defined in the scriptures as not desiring anyone's wealth by thought, word, or deed, and not taking anyone's possessions, no matter how small, without their permission. When we obtain what we desire by honest means, our mind remains at peace, free of fear; whereas when we obtain what we desire by dishonest means, we lose our peace of mind and become victims of fear.

Not only does the act of stealing expend mental and physical energy, but the fear that is generated makes the mind agitated and restless. A thief may seem courageous, but his so-called courage is actually a form of fear. Moreover, having faith that stealing will provide our needs is weakness rather than faith, and developing stealing skills is a sign of foolishness rather than cleverness.

Even Saints are Thieves

Some people say that the words "thief" and "theft" are useless; that these words do not belong in the dictionary. They claim that because this entire world is the Lord's creation, everyone has equal right to what is in it. "Where is the question of stealing, if we are using our own things?" they say. "Since the whole world is one family, everything we acquire, either secretly or openly, belongs to our own relatives and is, therefore, ours."

Many people are totally convinced that this world is a large marketplace full of thieves; in many ways they are correct. Yet, there are different types of thieves: ordinary thieves, skilled thieves, and master thieves. Master thieves are called aristocrats, skilled thieves are called gentlemen, and ordinary thieves are called saints! Here, I cannot resist telling you a story.

Anecdote: The angel and the hyena

During medieval times, civil wars were rampant. In those days, kings used to erect forts to protect their towns and villages. The fortress gates would be opened in the early morning and closed every evening at fixed times. One day a traveler named Marvadi came to one of these villages. He saw the gates closing from a distance and he ran to get inside, but he was too late; they were closed tightly just as he arrived. He repeatedly begged the gate-keeper to open the gates, but to no avail. It was winter, too, and he was extremely cold. Not only that, but the surrounding forest was filled with fierce animals. However, this traveler was a country peddler, and his experience with such circumstances helped him pass the night safely even without the shelter of the fortress.

That night, however, was filled with suspense. There was a cemetary close to the spot where Marvadi slept. In the middle of the night, he was startled awake by a strange sound. By the light of the moon, he was able to see a hyena digging up a freshly buried corpse. In no time at all, that fierce animal had opened the grave and dragged the corpse away.

Soon it was daybreak, and the gates to the village were opened. As Marvadi prepared to leave the forest, a Muslim family came to offer flowers at the same grave that the hyena had dug up during the night. Seeing the open grave, a child who had come with his father said, "Father, why is the tomb empty? Where has grandfather gone?"

The father concealed his dispair, though he knew that an animal had stolen the corpse. To satisfy his child, however, he said, "An angel must have taken him away."

Marvadi heard them talking in Urdu, the language of the Muslims. Using his working knowledge of that language, he said, "Brother, I slept here overnight and saw a hyena come, dig up the body, and drag it away."

If the Muslim family were to believe that the corpse had actually been dragged away by a wild animal, they would have been upset. So to prevent this, the elder spokesman for the family raised his fist in anger and denied the traveler's statement.

But Marvadi was a practical man, so he toned down his statement a bit to avoid unnecessary trouble. Diplomatically, he replied, "Brother, let's not quarrel. It's just that we speak different languages. The word "hyena" in my language means "angel" in yours, so I merely made a mistake in translation. Still, however, the corpse was in fact taken by a hyena."

In this anecdote, Marvadi's last statement was the same as his first. Thus, just as he used the word hyena in two different ways, when someone in this world of thieves is referred to as an aristocrat, a gentleman, or a saint, he is still actually a thief.

Stealing is the religion of life: goldsmiths steal gold, blacksmiths steal iron, carpenters steal wood, tailors steal cloth, and teachers steal knowledge. We all develop thievery skills, and the one who becomes most supremely skillful is called a great yogi.

Even deities like Shiva, Vishnu, and Shakti incarnate as thieves. They steal too! Does it matter much whether they steal your mind or your money? They are thieves just the same. In fact, we could say that they are first class thieves, masters of the art of thievery, forerunners in the skill of stealing, and the supreme propagators of thievery.

Literature is one of the various forms of entertainment available today. All forms of entertainment have developed and prospered because of our pervasive and widespread entrapment in delusion. Eggplants grown on farms are different from eggplants shown in pictures; those from the farm can be eaten, but those in pictures can only be looked at.

Stealing was considered an art in India for ages. As illustrated in the story that follows, many arts involve inborn skills, and stealing is no exception.

Anecdote: The theft of a cloth

Since stealing was considered to be an art in ancient times, arrangements were often made to cultivate its expression. We must remember here, however, that it is one thing for an artist to develop a career as an artist, and another for a thief to make stealing his vocation in life. In ancient times, even kings and aristocrats taught their children the fine art of stealing to sharpen their intellect. In those days, if a theft could not be solved, the king would issue a proclamation of amnesty. The guilty thief, upon hearing this, would then fearlessly present himself to the state assembly and disclose the trick he used in committing the crime. He would be set free and given a reward of a specified number of gold coins.

Since stealing was considered an art, a seminar was once arranged on the subject during a state assembly. As the seminar ended, it was decided that an expert in the art of stealing should be questioned and asked to demonstrate his skills. The first name that occurred to the participants was that of a prosperous tailor in town, who was a favorite among the king's family. After the seminar, the king sent for him and said, "Mohanbhai, two days ago, we held a seminar on the art of stealing. Many participants nominated you as the leading expert in the art. Is this true?"

"Your Excellency," Mohanbhai replied with dignity, "having served your family for many years, I am naturally quite prosperous. Let it be clear that I have never stolen anything to acquire wealth but only to practice the art. No art can develop without practice. Stealing is unacceptable only if it is done for the sake of acquiring wealth and not practiced as an art."

The king replied in a friendly way, "It is all right if you want to steal for the sake of the art, but what would you do if I ordered you not to steal at all?"

"You are the king," Mohanbhai respectfully replied, "and you are powerful. I would honor your command. Nevertheless, since I am an artist, I must say that even if I could not steal a lot, I would always get away with a little bit."

The king replied, "And if I would not allow you to do even a small amount of stealing, then what?"

"Then, I must confess," Mohanbhai said, "that I could not be considered an expert artist if I could not steal at least something anyway."

"Then we will have to conduct an experiment," the king said. The princess is about to be married. Many dresses need to be made for the wedding. I will have you sew the dresses, but you must do so under the watchful eyes of the state inspectors."

"As you desire," Mohanbhai consented.

The king ordered the cloth for the dresses. Mohanbhai sat in the palace under the close observation of the inspectors and began sewing the dresses. At the end of each day, the king ordered the inspectors to check Mohanbhai's pockets before he went home. One day, Mohanbhai's twelve-year-old daughter and eight-year-old son came to the palace. As the two stood at the door, the daughter said loudly, "Father, my brother will not stay at home. He's very mischievous and bothers everybody."

"Go away!" Mohanbhai said. "Take him home! Can't you see that I am busy?"

"But he wants five rupees," the daughter said.

One of the inspectors was surprised. "Five rupees?" he said. "Why does he need so much money? Mohanbhai! I think you've spoiled this child with too much affection. Otherwise, why would this little boy ask for five rupees?"

"Father," the child immediately said, "Give me five rupees!"

"I didn't bring any money with me," Mohanbhai said. "Go home! I will give you some when I come."

"No! No! Rupees!" the boy said.

Mohanbhai picked up his wooden tailor's gauge and threw it at his son, but he did it in such a manner as to scare the boy and not to hurt him. "Are you going, or not?" Mohanbhai said.

"No! No! I want rupees!" his son insisted. In anger, Mohanbhai threw a shoe at his son. "This is the only kind of rupees I have!"

The inspector was afraid the child would be injured and said, "Mohanbhai, don't continue throwing things at your child. He may get hurt."

His son, however, kept the shoe and said, "I will only give back your shoe if you give me rupees."

"Oh really?" Mohanbhai said, "Then take these rupees!" And he threw his other shoe.

The two children ran away with the shoes. The inspector burst into laughter. "Mohanbhai," he said, "Today you will have to go home barefoot."

"I don't mind," Mohanbhai said, "It is enough that those kids are gone. I can't stand to be disturbed when I am work-

ing. From now on, I'm going to keep some stones here to make sure they stay away."

"Mohanbhai," the inspector said, "Don't keep stones with you or you may hurt the children."

"I know that," Mohanbhai said, "I will take care that I don't hurt them. But I must scold them in this manner or else they won't believe me."

When Mohanbhai had finished sewing the dresses for the wedding, the king called the inspectors and said, "Did you watch carefully to make sure that there was no stealing?"

"Yes, your Excellency," the inspectors said. "We checked his pockets every day before he went home. We are sure that he has not stolen anything."

Then the king called Mohanbhai. "Well, Mohanbhai," the king said, "Have you succeeded in your art or failed?"

Mohanbhai took out some stolen cloth and said, "By your grace, I have succeeded."

The king was pleased. "You are truly an expert at this art," he said. "How did you steal this cloth?"

"If you are really pleased," Mohanbhai said, "Give me a reward of 25,000 rupees in addition to my regular payment

for sewing the dresses, and I will disclose my secret."
The king agreed.

Mohanbhai described the whole incident with his two children and said that he had hidden the cloth in both shoes! The king's face lit up with a smile.

Yogic Secrets are Kept for the Protection of Yoga, Not for Stealing

One person may desire to be a yogi and another may strive to be a sanyasi, but no one wants to be considered a thief. Whenever we conceal something from another person, however, we become thieves.

Yet, not everything that is concealed is stolen. For example, the science of yoga is extremely esoteric, and its secrets are always concealed from the undeserving. However, the great yogis are protecting truth rather than committing theft. They protect the truth for those who deserve it.

Some time ago, beloved Vinit Muni asked me a question. The question he asked concerned an advanced stage of yoga sadhana that was beyond his present experience, so I did not answer it. He is a sadhak on the path of nivritti marga and has practiced sadhana for the last four years. He is my disciple and my son; whatever is mine is his also. And yet this knowledge of yoga is spiritual knowledge rather than wealth. It is only given gradually as one develops the capacity to understand it experientially.

The spiritual seeker's face radiates with joy when an esoteric secret is revealed to him through his personal experience in sadhana. This is the supreme means to realize sadhana's esoteric truths. Usually a description of the most important yogic experiences is available in one of the scriptures. Since a Sadguru is generous and just rather than selfish and cunning, he conceals nothing from a deserving disciple. But, the disciple must reach a particular stage of sadhana before the Sadguru will reveal the secret of that stage. If for some important reason he must reveal the secret early, the

Sadguru will only give a clue, because the disciple can only realize that particular secret after attaining that stage.

One constantly faces delusions in yoga sadhana, because his emotions are heightened. These delusions are one type of obstacle which all sadhaks must contend with until they attain samadhi. In my sadhana, also, this type of obstacle has continually occurred. I have been deluded in my sadhana, because I considered these experiences to be significant yogic experiences. But as my sadhana has progressed, I have discovered how to discriminate between a true major experience of sadhana and a delusion by evaluating the experience over and over again. Now, I consider an experience to be a major attainment only after it passes my final test.

There is a vast difference between bonafide and misinterpreted yogic experiences; yet, hyperemotionality has led even the best seekers astray. The spiritual seeker must keep this fact clear in his mind: genuine and nongenuine attainments only appear to be similar because of the seeker's emotional attachment. In fact, these attainments are as different as day is from night. The seeker is simply deluded if he believes otherwise.

If a seeker does not allow such delusions to lead him astray, and if he continues on the correct path, sooner or later he will see that the experience was a delusion rather than a true yogic experience. However, if the seeker follows his misinterpretation and takes the wrong path, he will continue to believe that the delusion is real. Seekers who are led astray in this way are behaving contrary to the ultimate truth. Consequently, any scriptures written by them are erroneous, and anyone who practices sadhana under their guidance is led down the path to delusion. The major difference between true scriptures and deluded scriptures is that the true scriptures of the great realized yogis make it patently obvious that the nivritti path is only for an extraordinarily great person. On the other hand, the scriptures of a deluded yogi represent the nivritti path as a social religion which everyone can practice.

We can gather good thoughts either by listening to inspiring orators or by studying the works of excellent authors. However, when we speak or write these same thoughts, we should express gratitude towards their originator, or it is a theft of thoughts. Yes, we steal not just for material wealth but also for fame; that is, we steal the thoughts and conduct of another. This is like a crow wearing the feathers of a peacock.

Stealing is immoral, and nonstealing is moral. Anyone who desires to travel on the path to the Lord must practice morality.

Concentration is essential to thieves—both while planning and while stealing. But this type of concentration is a doorway to spiritual downfall rather than spiritual ascent. *The yogic scriptures provide instructions for concentration of a pure nature. Yoga sadhana must be done with effort in an appropriate place. During the day we are usually engaged in rajasic or tamasic concentration, so naturally we don't need a meditation room for that! When we engage in these forms of concentration while sitting in meditation, however, feelings of attachment and hatred quickly develop and potentiate the concentration.*

Causing disturbance in someone's mind is a subtle form of violence. Thus, stealing is a form of violence since it disturbs the mind of our victim. Moreover, not only do thieves need to act dishonestly to steal something, but they must lie to conceal their theft. Their possessions are consequently contaminated, and they break their vow of nonattachment and nonstealing. Thus, one simple theft is enough to destroy the entire fortress of spiritual discipline. I will tell you a story which I hope will illuminate this subject for you.

Anecdote: Dala Tarvadi

Anyone can write or speak religious thoughts, but not everyone can practice them. Religious behavior requires austerity, and anyone who cannot consistently practice austerity cannot absorb religion. To be religious is to be an ascetic.

Steam is generated from water and heat, and, yet, no work can be performed with that steam if it is not properly channeled. Likewise, thoughts that are not channeled into behavior remain impotent.

There once was a man named Dala Tarvadi who lived in a small village. He had read a few religious scriptures. One day, without any apparent reason, Tarvadi took a walk to the outskirts of the village. Suddenly, he noticed a small garden owned by a man named Vashrambhai and walked over to see what he had planted this year. In the distance, he saw Vashrambhai himself, tending his garden.

Tarvadi called out loudly, "Hey Vashrambhai, how are you?"

"I'm fine," replied Vashrambhai casually, "What brings you out this way, Tarvadi?"

"I had a little work at the outskirts of the village," said Dala Tarvadi. "I happened to see your garden and thought I would go and see what you had planted. What have you put in this year?

"Vegetables," replied Vashrambhai. He took Dala Tarvadi on a tour of the entire garden. Then he said, "Here, take home a few of these eggplants; they're great!"

Tarvadi gratefully took the eggplants and went home. That evening he prepared the eggplants for supper and liked them very much. Two or three days later he remembered those delicious eggplants again; but he knew that Vashrambhai would not give them away free every time. And yet, he did not want to pay the expensive price for them either. Engrossed in thoughts about the eggplants, once again Dala Tarvadi walked to the outskirts of the village. He looked around to make sure that the orchard was empty. Then he trespassed into the garden and went to the small mound where the eggplants were growing. But just as he was about to take some eggplants, he remembered a line from the scriptures: "If you take anything without the owner's permission, you are stealing."

Tarvadi knew that the owner was not around and that even if he was, he wouldn't just give away expensive eggplants for nothing. It took a few minutes to wrestle with his conscience, but eventually Dala Tarvadi devised a way to take the eggplants without cost and still feel that he was observing the scriptures. He softly said to the garden, "Oh Garden! Sister Garden."

But how could a garden of vines, vegetables, and trees give a response?

Dala Tarvadi spoke in reply for the garden in a feminine voice: "What do you want, Dala Tarvadi?"

"May I take two or three eggplants?" Tarvadi said in his own voice.

Then again he replied in a feminine voice, "Sure, brother, help yourself! Take ten or eleven." So Dala Tarvadi took home as many eggplants as he wanted.

After learning the exact time at which Vashrambhai went home and the garden was empty for the day, Tarvadi began to come for eggplants every evening.

Eventually, Vashrambhai realized that someone was stealing his eggplants. So, one day he hid in the garden when he normally would have gone home. Soon, he spied Dala Tarvadi come and start picking eggplants in his usual manner, taking permission from the garden. Vashrambhai came out from his hiding place and caught him.

Dala Tarvadi was embarrassed and ashamed, but Vashrambhai did not scold or hit him. Instead, he tied a rope around Tarvadi and lowered him into the well. When the water came up to Tarvadi's neck, Vashrambhai called out, "Brother well. Oh, brother well!"

Then Vashrambhai changed his voice, and spoke in reply for the well. "Hello, Vashrambhai! What did you say?"

"Shall I dunk him two or three times?" Vashrambhai said with his regular voice.

Changing back to the voice of the well, he said, "Oh brother, dunk him ten or eleven times!" So, with the consent of the well, Vashrambhai dunked Dala Tarvadi eleven times before pulling him out of the well.

Dala Tarvadi was totally exhausted and unconscious, for he had swallowed lots of water. Eventually, after he had pulled himself together, he went home with soaking wet clothes and drenched in despondency. He had learned his lesson, and from that day on gave up his habit of stealing eggplants!

There are five scripturally prescribed spiritual disciplines: nonviolence, truth, celibacy, nonattachment, and nonstealing. When any of these are broken, the mind becomes restless. While a flame in a windy place flickers unsteadily, a mind in the shelter of the spiritual disciplines burns on steadily.

Chapter 5

Nonattachment

Nonattachment and Attachment	69
Anecdote: The old man and the mango tree	69
Nonattachment Comes Gradually	71
Anecdote: The squirrel and the bridge	72
Anecdote: The nonattached yogi Bhatrihari	74
Anecdote: The long-haired saint	76
Anecdote: The mad saint	77
Anecdote: The laborer and the three stones	80

20 July 1977
Wednesday, 6:15 a.m.
Kripalu Yoga Retreat
Summit Station, PA

Nonattachment and attachment

In my last two discourses I presented thoughts on nonviolence and truth. Today I will express some thoughts on nonattachment, or aparigraha. Attachment and nonattachment are antonyms. The Sanskrit "parigraha" means "to store or accumulate with strong attachment," "to cling firmly to," or "to fasten completely to." Since the prefix "a" means "not," "aparigraha," therefore, has the opposite meaning: "to firmly give up" and "not to accumulate or hoard."

I will discuss nonattachment as it pertains to the needs of three types of spiritual seekers: ordinary, intermediate, and ideal. A moderate degree of nonattachment can be attained by an intermediate seeker; true nonattachment can be attained only by the ideal seeker. This highest seeker is looking only for liberation, and his sole desire is to cling to the feet of the Lord. He therefore firmly renounces his attachment to the illusory world. However, since he still desires liberation, he remains attached to nonattachment! Because one can practice sadhana only according to one's capacity, seekers beginning their spiritual journey must start from a state of high attachment and gradually travel in the direction of nonattachment.

Anecdote: The old man and the mango tree

The concept of public welfare or social service differs from that of nonattachment. Social service in the truest sense can be performed only by the greatest masters who have taken the vow of nonattachment. The average person can perform little true social service, but his service can at least be considered the *start* of nonattachment.

There is a story I'd like to recount about a young man named Kumaril. Kumaril had a garden in the open courtyard of his home. One day, as he entered the garden, he saw his elderly uncle, Padmakant, busy at work. As Kumaril came closer, he saw that his uncle was energetically planting seedlings. It was obvious that Padmakant, even at the age of ninety, loved to work. Kumaril was impressed by his uncle's industriousness.

"Uncle," Kumaril said respectfully, "what are you planting?"

Padmakant stopped working and looked up at Kumaril, smiling. "My son," he said, "I'm planting mango trees."

Seeing about fifteen small mango plants, Kumaril asked, "You're planting so many?"

"There are only fifteen," Padmakant remarked.

"Don't you think that fifteen are too many for this garden?" Kumaril inquired.

"No, it's all right," Padmakant said. "There's no other place to plant them."

"They will bear lots of mangoes," Kumaril added as a compliment to his uncle.

"Thank you," Padmakant replied. "May that thought come true."

"But uncle," Kumaril said as he began to laugh, "you are ninety years old! When will these mango trees bear fruit?"

"In twelve years," Padmakant answered.

"But you may leave your body before then; why are you doing all this work?"

"Son, I am sure that I will be home with God before these mango trees bear fruit," said Padmakant. "But I am planting these trees for others, not for myself. For ninety years, I have eaten mangoes from trees which had been planted by other people. Now I want to plant some mango trees so that others may eat from trees I have planted."

Kumaril observed nonattachment in his uncle's feelings and began to understand that one who gathers for himself is a worldly person, while one who gathers for others has renounced his worldly attachments.

Nonattachment Comes Gradually

When a schoolteacher solves a math problem on the blackboard, does he solve it for himself? No, he solves it for his students. Nonattachment grows whenever we give knowledge or perform any selfless action. I love to teach very much. Even the ancient seers of India continued teaching after they had become fully liberated. They did not teach because they were attached to the scriptures. But why, then, did they teach? They were not actually performing any actions in the usual sense. Their actions were actually a form of inaction.

Any action which is not motivated by selfish desire is actually considered a form of inaction. For example, any action which is performed for the love of God or the public welfare, dedicated to Brahma, or spontaneously inspired by the Lord is "action in inaction" and the best of all forms of nonattachment.

We may use any action to acquire happiness either for ourselves or for others. When we perform actions for others, however, we receive greater joy. This heightened joy is not simply joy in the usual sense; it is, in fact, the grace of the Lord.

A person begins to recognize his own individual existence a few years after birth. At the moment he begins to distinguish between "yours" and "mine," he plants the roots of attachment. Even if he had unlimited power and could accumulate everything he ever wanted, several large cities could not hold it all! With all our attachments, if someone approached us and asked us to consider practicing nonattachment, we would scorn his suggestion.

It is as difficult to move from attachment to nonattachment as it is to move from the earth to the sky. Nonattachment simply cannot be achieved in a single bound; only a gradual, step-by-step ascent is possible. As we are more and more able to absorb a principle, our behavior changes gradually, and our personal effort becomes easier. If a thousand pounds of grain were piled in front of us, do you think we could eat it all in one day? Of course not. However, if we had one hundred years to live, we could eat twenty piles that big.

A person should practice nonattachment as best he can, whether he is a worldly person or a renunciate.

Anecdote: The squirrel and the bridge

In the ancient allegory of the *Ramayan*, when Lord Ram received the news from courageous Hanuman that Sita had been kidnapped by Ravan, the king of Lanka, and that she was being kept in Ashoka Vana, he immediately decided to invade Lanka.

Ram's army of monkeys came to the ocean and at once began building a bridge to cross it. A squirrel living nearby watched the huge army of monkeys arriving. She observed them for awhile and soon discovered that there was one very special man among them. Each morning the entire army would pay their respects to him by bowing down; afterwards, they would begin their daily task of building the bridge. One day, the squirrel received the audience of that great man; she developed a feeling in her heart of deep love and felt a desire to serve him. Since the bridge building seemed an act of service to this great man, she willingly joined in the task.

The squirrel very carefully observed how the monkeys were constructing the bridge. Before the monkeys moved each of the large rocks needed for the bridge, they would chant the name of Ram and the rock would begin to float on the water. Because she did not have the strength to lift the huge rocks, the squirrel was sad; yet, her strong desire to serve gave birth to an idea. She went close to the bridge and happily began rolling in the sand on the seashore. Each time she performed this action, sand would stick to her fur. Each time she would place all the sand between the large rocks on the bridge. She could make twenty or thirty trips with sand in the same amount of time that it took a monkey to place one rock on the bridge. When the monkeys saw her loving, eager service, they were all so moved that they forgot the difficulty of their own labor and hurried to bring the rocks to the bridge. The tiny squirrel had soon inspired the entire army to work more efficiently.

This story illustrates two qualities of those who love: (1) only those who truly love themselves can perceive true love, and (2) lovers see more love in others than in themselves. Thus, the monkeys felt that the squirrel had deeper devotion for Ram than they did. They perceived her true love and received more joy from observing her devotion than from the devotion in their own hearts. The strength of one's devotion will determine whether it manifests partially or totally. True devotion, however, is always total, no matter where it is displayed.

Soon the sun set, and the monkeys stopped their work. Night came, and the entire army of monkeys bowed to Lord Ram and sat in front of him. Many of the monkeys were eager to talk about the squirrel's loving service, but they sat silently and looked at the courageous Hanuman for permission to speak. The squirrel was also in silent attendance. Hiding herself at the feet of Hanuman so that no one could see her, she gazed continuously and rapturously at Lord Ram. Naturally, the wise Hanuman knew what she was up to but acted as if nothing was happening.

"Lord," said one monkey eagerly, "today a tiny squirrel destroyed the sense of ego in our devotion to you. We were carrying huge rocks, and she was carrying sand. She continually rolled in the sand on the seashore so that sand stuck to her; she brought the sand to the bridge and placed it between the large stones. In the time we took to bring one rock, she had brought twenty or thirty loads of sand. We experienced boundless joy today at the sight of her loving service."

After hearing this tale, Lord Ram expressed his happiness at the squirrel's service. Suddenly, Hanuman gently picked up the squirrel and lovingly placed her at the feet of the Lord. All the monkeys shouted with joy. The gracious Lord stroked her tiny body. His fingers left impressions on her fur; it was as if the unseen grace of the Lord had become visible.

Like the squirrel, we are all tiny seekers. Even if we cannot attain enough nonattachment to carry big boulders, we will definitely progress if we carry a bit of sand. Start by awakening devotion to yoga. Actually, devotion to yoga is devotion to Ram, and devotion to Ram is devotion to yoga.

We are born with attachment, so naturally we want to accumulate things. Now that we have accumulated so much, we have a list of countless attachments in our memory. Under these circumstances, from what door will the poor idea of nonattachment enter our mind? Fortunately, nonattachment is extremely patient and tolerant. It has been standing outside the door of our mind for many lifetimes. It will enter whenever we call it, and then the dawn of knowledge, devotion, and yoga will break.

Anecdote: The nonattached yogi Bhatrihari

When a spiritual seeker's only aim is to attain the Supreme Being, nonattachment in its truest form is accomplished spontaneously without any special efforts. Just as any traveler who is heading west is naturally going away from the east, any seeker who is heading toward liberation is naturally moving away from wordly illusion. When seekers desiring liberation begin yoga sadhana, any previous impressions of attachment remaining in their minds—however few—begin to manifest and create a little disturbance. But the seeker frees himself from them through the power of discrimination, which increases daily as his mind and body purify. The more his love for the Lord increases, the more his love for worldly illusions decreases.

Once upon a time, in ancient India, there was a very valiant king named Bhatrihari. Even today he is regarded as one of the best Sanskrit poets and yogis, and his kingdom, Ujjayini, remains a place of pilgrimage. After he had renounced his throne, Bhatrihari practiced yoga sadhana for a long time and finally achieved samadhi. The great yogis who have achieved this union with God truly personify the practice of nonattachment. Some of them do not even feel the need to wear clothes. Their nonattachment has blossomed to such an extent that they can detach their consciousness from their body and mind and reside solely in the soul.

Once upon a time, the great yogi Bhatrihari came to a cemetery while traveling. When he sat down to rest under a canopy of trees, he suddenly became aware that the loincloth he was wearing, which was made of bark, was torn in several places. "This should be sewn," he thought. So he stood up and searched around until he found two thorns. He used one thorn to make a hole in the end of the other. But when he tried to thread his crude needle with fiber from the bark of a tree, he was unable to see well enough in the fast-approaching twilight.

At the same moment, Lord Shiva was traveling across the sky with Mother Parvati. While trying to thread the needle, Bhatrihari was chanting, "Om namah Shivaya, Om namah Shivaya, Om namah Shivaya." It was his usual practice to chant thus while performing any task. The words of the chant fell upon the ears of Mother Parvati, and she looked down and spotted Bhatrihari. Mother Parvati was a perfect devotee of Lord Shiva, and she loved Shiva's devotees as much as she loved Shiva himself. For this reason, she desired to meet Bhatrihari.

The omniscient Lord Shiva immediately knew her desire.

Mother Parvati humbly said, "My Lord, one of your devotees is sitting alone under a tree. If you will kindly come down with me, I would like to meet him."

"He is not worth meeting," replied Lord Shiva.

"But he is one of your perfect devotees," exclaimed Mother Parvati with surprise. "How can you say he's not worth meeting?"

Both of them landed on the earth and stood behind Bhatrihari; but Mother Parvati wanted to face him.

Lord Shiva whispered softly into Mother Parvati's ear, "Say whatever you want to him."

"Bhatrihari, my son," she said, "I am Parvati, your mother. I have come down here with your father, Lord Shiva, to meet you. We are both standing behind you."

Bhatrihari neither replied nor turned his head; he simply kept on sewing.

Mother Parvati found this behavior strange, as well as rude. She rebuked him saying, "It was my wish to come down to earth just to meet you, yet you won't even turn to look at me."

"Don't talk so much!" replied Bhatrihari. "Have you grown so old that you don't remember anything?"

Bhatrihari's every word was filled with tender love for the mother; this pleased her heart fully. "It's true that I have grown old," said Mother Parvati. "But I don't believe what you say about my not remembering anything."

"You will believe it when you hear what I am about to say," said Bhatrihari. "So listen. Aren't you everywhere? You are in front of me; you are behind me; you are above and beneath me. You are everywhere. You are in my heart, my sight, and my speech. So tell me, how can I believe your statement that you are standing behind me? I can even see you in the hole in this thorn and in the fiber of this bark. Why should I turn around when you are right here in front of me?"

Mother Parvati's heart opened with love. She suddenly understood Lord Shiva's statement that Bhatrihari was not worth meeting. "My son," she said with affection, "I am very pleased with you. Ask any boon you want."

"You are talking nonsense again," Bhatrihari said with indifference. He didn't even turn around as he spoke. "OK, if you insist on granting a boon, take this thorn and thread it for me. How can I disobey your order?"

Mother Parvati threaded the thorn with the fiber and then expressed her sadness. "Don't you want anything from me?" she asked.

"Just go away and don't bother me," said Bhatrihari. "The fact that I have attained you is the greatest boon I can ever have. I don't believe that a greater boon exists in this world. You are boons, and boons are you. What happiness can I possibly receive from any other boon?"

Now, that kind of nonattachment is the nonattachment experienced by the great yogis.

Anecdote: The long-haired saint

The story I will now relate is about a saint of medium caliber. Even saints come in different qualities. This saint, however, was the best of the medium caliber saints and practiced a high level of renunciation. He never stayed anywhere for more than two or three days, nor did he ever choose the direction of his travel. He simply moved wherever his feet took him.

One morning, Laturia Maharaj was walking on a road. He gave no thought at all to where he was headed. The wind was blowing fiercely against his back, and his long hair kept blowing in his face. He had to repeatedly brush his hair away from his face with his hands, but to no avail.

Finally, he reached the limit of his patience. He abruptly turned around and faced the strong wind with fire in his eyes, but the wind ignored him. He began to walk again, and after another unsuccessful bout with trying to keep his hair out of his face, he turned around a second time; but the wind ignored his threatening gaze again. Exasperated, he stopped again and muttered to himself, "This silly wind is causing mischief today. I will have to straighten it out or it will continue to cause problems."

So, Laturia Maharaj turned around and started to walk directly into the wind. With a triumphant smile on his face, he said, "Hello, my friend! Now do your mischief!" The wind now blew his hair behind him, away from his face! So ends the story of Laturia Maharaj, the long-haired saint.

Anecdote: The mad saint

One day, a renunciate saint came to a large city. He noticed that a concrete road had been built beside a dusty dirt road. An old, broken bamboo basket lay beside the dirt road; he picked it up and began filling it with dirt and emptying it onto the concrete road. After a few hours, he had a huge mound of dirt on the concrete road.

Anyone watching his actions would have considered him really crazy; and crazy he was. But his madness was from practicing yoga rather than from mental disorder. He was suffering from the madness of love and devotion. He was a yoga seeker, but he had been led astray.

In yoga sadhana it is absolutely essential to have the guidance of a Sadguru who is adept at yoga. If a seeker practices yoga sadhana without this guidance, at some point in his sadhana he becomes crazy with love and leaves the sadhana. However, since this madness is very different from mental disorder, the seeker's typical behavior appears very saintly. We receive a glimpse of his saintly personality in his usual speech and conduct.

Later that afternoon, the renunciate saint finished making an enormous pile of dirt right in the middle of the concrete road. Then, he sat in the lotus position on top of the pile as if he had worked all these hours just to sit there like this. Just then, the king's procession came down the same road. Usually, the roads on which the king's procession traveled were decided in advance so that the state officers could prepare the way. But today the king had suddenly changed his mind and had taken this new road.

As the king's attendants rode ahead to clear the road, they saw the large pile of dirt in the middle of the road with an apparently crazy person sitting on top. Since they could not possibly clear the way in time for the king to pass, the only thing they could do was ask the "mad person" sitting there to move. The chief of the horsemen looked at the "mad person" and concluded he was a saint. Since everyone knew that the king was religious and never ridiculed any saint, the chief horseman approached the saint and humbly said, "The king is coming."

The saint gazed indifferently at the attendant. "Who?" he yawned.

"The king of this city." replied the horseman.

The saint continued to appear unimpressed. "The king is coming? So let him come. There is enough room for him to pass."

"But he is the king," the horseman persisted. "He should not have to suffer the humiliation of squeezing past one of his subjects. You should get up and move."

"Me get up? Why should I get up?" quibbled the saint. "If there's a king coming, then I am entitled to remain here, since I am an emperor! There's plenty of room for him to pass by."

It was not possible to move the saint from the pile of dirt without using force. Yet, the king had previously ordered that nobody should be harassed during his processions. The horseman returned to the king and explained: "Your Highness! There is a saint sitting on top of a pile of dirt in the middle of the road. When I told him to get up, he said, 'I am an emperor. The king has plenty of room to pass if he wants.'"

The king said with a smile, "All right, we will pass by."

The procession continued. When they came to the saint, the king halted the procession and came down from atop his elephant. Approaching the saint, he offered pranams and humbly asked, "Are you an emperor?"

"Yes," replied the saint. "Let there be no doubt about it."

"What's the difference between a king and an emperor?" the king asked.

"A king is a prisoner of a small or a large state," the saint said. "He is not free to leave his state or his palace and live in another state. He cannot travel alone. Twenty-five to fifty people have to carry him from one place to another.

"I am an emperor. I can move about in any state whenever I want unaccompanied by anyone."

The king was extremely pleased with the saint's reply. He had no further questions for the saint, but he continued the discussion for the pure joy of hearing the saint's remarks. "A king has vast wealth," said the king. "You are an emperor. You must have even more wealth."

"A king is a prisoner; thus, he is unhappy," explained the saint. "Only one who is unhappy accumulates wealth. Only one who has expenses needs wealth. I don't have any expenses, so I don't need any money. I do not hoard or store anything either. An emperor is someone who has no possessions and is unattached to possessions. No one in the world is wealthier than he is."

The king enjoyed this satsang very much. He said with a laugh, "Surely, you must have a large kingdom, and if so, naturally, you must have a large army."

"Army?" the saint retorted with a frown. "Why an army? Only the person who has enemies needs an army. I don't have any enemies. Why should I need an army?"

The king was speechless; he bowed in respect to the saint.

"Keep your bows," said the saint. "They are useless to me."

The king left feeling very pleased and happy. He had received much food for thought. The saint closed his eyes and resumed his meditation while sitting atop the pile of dirt.

How can a king impress someone who wants nothing? This degree of nonattachment belongs only to saints; worldly people can be impressed by anybody: kings, aristocrats, ordinary people, and even paupers. They must progress gradually toward nonattachment as much as they are able.

Anecdote: The laborer and the three stones

A rich man was building a temple on the summit of a high mountain. He needed to have three large stones carried up the mountainside. After deciding how much he would pay for the labor, the rich man gave the task to a certain laborer. The laborer was strong, and he eagerly started up the mountain carrying all three stones at once. After climbing for a while, however, he became tired and felt the need to lighten his load. He left one stone on a ledge and continued climbing with the two remaining stones. However, after climbing for a distance, he felt the need to lighten his load even more. So, he left the second stone on another ledge. After that, his load was much lighter and within his carrying capacity. He was able to successfully complete his task.

Glossary

ashram—a religious hermitage or abode of tapas
bhajan—a devotional song
bhakti yoga—the yoga of devotion
brahmacharya—celibacy; giving up all sexual activity in thought, word, or deed; literally, "movement toward the Lord."
bhoga—hedonism
gunas—the three qualities of chitta (mindstuff): sattva guna, rajo guna, tamo guna. Their individual qualities are as follows:
    sattva guna—an illuminated state of mind characterized by purity; binds the person to joy, bliss, and perfect health. Sattva guna gives rise to knowledge, and persons established in this guna grow and develop in goodness and wisdom. In this state, there is the beginning of stability of the sexual fluid. This state of mind dawns on the threshold of achieving sabij samadhi.
    rajo guna—an action-oriented state of mind characterized by strong emotions, desires, and attachments of every kind. This state binds the person to action and gives rise to greed. Persons bound by this guna experience average, ordinary evolution.
    tamo guna—a dull state of mind characterized by ignorance and lethargy. This state binds the person to qualities of indolence, sleep, and negligence, and gives rise to errors and mistakes. Persons bound by this guna tend to deteriorate or sink downwards into lower tendencies.
jagadguru—supreme guru, guru of the entire world.
jnana yoga—yoga of knowledge

karma yoga—yoga of action

nivritti dharma—sadhana for only the most advanced sadhaks; seekers on this path use the potentials of prana to achieve the fourth and final goal of life: liberation; also called nishkam sadhana, sahaj yoga, kundalini yoga, sadhana of prana.

pravritti dharma—sadhana for either evolved worldly seekers or advanced seekers of religion; seekers on this path use the potentials of the mind to achieve the first three objectives in life: religion, wealth, and passion; also called sakama (with desire) sadhana and sadhana of chitta.

rajasic—see gunas

Ramayana—ancient Indian epic which depicts the adventures of Ram.

rupee—Indian currency worth approximately $.12

sabij samadhi—samadhi with mind or with the seed of desire; samadhi having subject-object or knower-known distinction. The seed of existence of the world (external and internal) is the sexual fluid (semen/ovum). The jurisdiction of sabij (with seed) samadhi continues as long as sexual fluid ejaculates and as long as chitta and prana remain unsteady.

sadhak—a practitioner of yoga

sadhana—spiritual practices

swami—member of an order of sanyasis

tamasic—see gunas

virya—sexual fluid

Swami Kripalvanandji

His Holiness Swami Shri Kripalvanandji, affectionately known as Bapuji, was one whose whole life was an expression of his burning desire for God-realization. He was born in 1913 to poor yet devout Brahmin parents in Gujurat, India. From an unusually early age he loved to spend time in worship and devotion and developed remarkable talents in the fields of literature and music. Still, he felt unfulfilled. His desire for union with God was so intense, and his attempts to reach it so frustrating, that by the age of 19 he had come close to suicide three times. It was as he determinedly planned his fourth attempt that he was saved and guided onto the highest path of yoga by the compassionate master who was to become his guru, Dadaji.

Dadaji's deep love won Bapuji's heart. When he witnessed Dadaji's miraculous yogic powers, his mind was won over too, and he was filled with renewed hope of satisfying his unquenchable desire for God-realization. At Dadaji's request, Bapuji moved into Dadaji's ashram and began the close personal training that was to change his life.

After eight months of teaching, Dadaji gave Bapuji special yogic initiation, first requiring him to spend 40 days in total seclusion and silence, fasting on water, meditating, and chanting mantra. These were hard disciplines for a youth of 19, but Dadaji's great love for Bapuji enabled him to succeed. When he received initiation, Dadaji told him: "My son, my blessing to you is that you will become the world's greatest yogacharya." This blessing indeed came true.

When Bapuji had been with his guru only 1¼ years, Dadaji mysteriously disappeared. Though he had many devoted disciples, none had been able to discover his true name, much less where he had come from or where he had gone. Bapuji was left to pursue his way alone in the world, supported by his guru's last promise that Bapuji would see

him again when he had finally renounced all worldly desires. Nearly ten years later, Bapuji finally took initiation as a swami, a renunciate monk. He traveled throughout western India, teaching the scriptures and turning men's hearts toward God. In doing so, his natural gifts as a scholar, orator, musician, and poet flowered. Bapuji was so eloquent and inspiring that many of his listeners were moved to donate gifts of money, all of which he channeled towards the building of schools and temples for the further enlightenment of his countrymen.

After eight years spent in this manner, during which Bapuji meditated constantly on his guru and practiced his teachings devotedly, he and Dadaji reunited in a remarkable way. It was in 1952, during a pilgrimage, that Dadaji appeared to him with his true yogic body in the form of a beautiful youth. Without revealing his complete identity, Dadaji explained that he had taken on a normal human form for 1¾ years simply to be able to teach Bapuji personally. Two years later, Dadaji again appeared to Bapuji to encourage and guide him in his sadhana. It was at this time that Bapuji began his intense ten-hours-a-day practice of Kundalini meditation, a practice which he has maintained to his final days.

In 1955, Bapuji finally discovered his guru's complete historical identity during a visit to Kayavarohan, ancient India's great center of spiritual learning. Bapuji was taken into a temple where he was shown a large stone lingam, carved into which was the form of a young, seated yogi. In a flash of transcendental realization, he recognized it as his guru: Lord Lakulish (Bhagwan Brahmeshvar), 28th incarnation of Lord Shiva who had reincarnated in the 2nd century B.C. to restore Kayavarohan to its former glory and spiritual power.

Later, during meditation, Bapuji saw visions of Kayavarohan at the height of its flowering. He received a divine command to restore it yet again as a spiritual center, not only for India but for the whole world. Though a penniless swami, Bapuji bowed to divine will, and now Kayavarohan is rising again from the ashes like a phoenix and assuming a new and glorious future as an international center for spiritual enlightenment through the study of yoga, world scriptures, music, and many other related disciplines.

In addition to overseeing the restoration of Kayavarohan, Bapuji continued his brilliant work as a scholar and writer as well as his dedication to his most demanding sadhana. For twelve years he practiced total silence and for the ten years following he spoke only on rare, special occasions. The only exception to this extraordinary life was his arrival in the United States in 1977 where he was so struck by the openness of the aspiring seekers who greeted him that he delivered the series of lectures from which these volumes flow.

At the end of that first summer in America, Bapuji returned to seclusion and silence, residing at the ashram named for him by his close disciple Yogi Amrit Desai. He taught a few chosen disciples, wrote, continued his intense schedule of meditation, and once a week gave brief darshans for the hundreds who came to be in his presence. In September, 1981, Bapuji returned to India and, on December 29 of that year, left his body. For yoga masters such as Bapuji, this is known as *mahasamadhi*—his final merging into oneness with God. To honor Bapuji's memory and continue his work, a temple and ashram are being constructed at his burial site in Malav, Gujarat Province.

Books by and about Swami Kripalvanandji.

* *Science of Meditation.* Swami Kripalvanandji. Based on his personal experiences, a comprehensive and definitive work on all forms and stages of meditation.

  Asana and Mudra. Swami Kripalvanandji. A basic, detailed text on the physiology and psychology of hatha yoga. Soon to be released in English.

  Commentary on the Hatha Yoga Pradipika. Swami Shri Kripalvanandji. The first commentary on this ancient yogic scripture in over 800 years to be written from a great master's personal experience in the highest stage of enlightenment. Soon to be released in English.

* *Bapuji in America: Darshans at Kripalu Ashram.* A commemorative collection of Swami Kripalvanandji's biography, teachings, and stories.

* *Light from Guru to Disciple.* Rajarshi Muni. The inspiring and incredible account of Swami Kripalvanandji's life history, focusing on the discipleship and yogic training of this enlightened master.

* *Yoga Experiences.* Rajarshi Muni. A fascinating account of the many unusual experiences encountered during Kundalini Shaktipat meditation, written by one of Swami Kripalvanandji's closest disciples.

* Currently available through Kripalu Center.

For further information:
Kripalu Center
P.O. Box 793
Lenox, MA 01240

Index

Action
  as inaction, 71
Adolescents
  sensual lifestyles, 13
Anecdotes
  celibacy: Vasavdatta meets Upgupatta, 14-19
  love: The slave and the lion, 30-34
  nonattachment: The laborer and the three stones, 80
  nonattachment: The long-haired saint, 77-80
  nonattachment: The mad saint, 77-80
  nonattachment: The nonattached yogi Bhatrihari, 74-76
  nonattachment: The old man and the mango tree, 69-70
  nonattachment: The squirrel & the bridge, 72-74
  nonstealing: Dala Tarvadi, 64-66
  nonstealing: The angel & the hyena, 58-62
  nonstealing: The theft of a cloth, 58-62
  Silence: The businessman of Bengalgranus & seclusion, 45-48
  speech, disciplined: A sweet joke, 50-52
  speech, discrimination in: Do not answer this notice, 49-50
Animals
  influenced by love, 29
Art
  stealing as, 58

Attachment
  roots planted in childhood, 71
  worldly person and, 71-72
  See also Nonattachment
Behavior
  restraint of, 43
Bhagavad Gita
  on disciplined speech, 50
  on passion, 4
Bhakti yoga
  purification process in, 23
Bhatrihari, yogi
  anecdote: The nonattached yogi Bhatrihari, 74-76
Brahmacharya. See Celibacy
Celibacy
  anecdote: Vasavdatta meets Upgupatta, 14-15
  ancient experiments based on yoga, 3
  ancient sages' scientific experiments, 3-4
  ancient vs modern concepts, 3-6
  definition, 9
  benefits of, 6-9
  effects of sensuous lifestyles on, 6-7
  effect of sports & exercise on, 6
  effects of dress & grooming on, 11-12
  effects of thoughts on, 12
  key to successful practice of, 10-11
  source of contemporary concepts, 3-5
  total believed impossible, 3-6

vow of, 8-9
  See also Passion; Restraint
Clothing
  type affects behavior, 11-12
Concentration
  types of, 64
Conduct
  in male-female relationships, 10-12
  loving with family, 25-27
  transforming good thoughts into, 26-27
  vicious & virtuous acts are result of concentration, 35
Dadaji. See Lakulish, Lord Shri
Deities
  incarnate as thieves, 58
Delusion
  constant obstacle in sadhana, 63
  in Bapuji's sadhana, 63
  See also Maya
Desai, Yogi Amrit
  advice from Bapuji as a boy, 28
Desire, sexual. See Passion
Disciple
  guru reveals secrets to deserving, 62
Divine Body
  evolution of, 13-14
Exercise
  effects on celibacy, 6
Family
  effects of violent speech in, 25-27
  entire world is one, 11, 41
  nonviolence in, 25-27, 35
  prescription for harmony in, 27
  root cause of conflicts in, 27
Freud, Sigmund
  concepts re: human sexuality, 5
Gita. See *Bhagavad Gita*
Guru
  revelation of secrets to disciple, 62
Ideals
  developing, 28-29

India
  celibacy experiments in ancient 3-4
  spiritual & physical sciences developed in, 3-4
Introspection
  leads to self-observation, 44
  silence, seclusion & meditation aids to, 44
Jnana yoga
  purification process in, 23
Karma yoga
  purification process in, 23
Knowledge, spiritual
  given according to capacity, 62-63
Kripalvanand, Swami Shri
  advice to re: ideals, 28
  advice to sadhaks re sadhana, 28-29
  biographical: advice re women, 11
  biographical: delusions in sadhana, 63
  biographical: practice of self-observation, 44
  biographical: speech, disciplined (anecdote), 50-52
Krishna, Lord Shri
  preachings on disciplined speech, 50
Lakulish, Lord Shri
  recognized by Bapuji, 85
Liberation
  ancient seers taught after attaining, 71
  nonattachment & seeker of, 69, 74
Lifestyle
  affects celibacy, 6-7, 13
Love
  anecdote: Vasavdatta meets Upgupatta, 14-19
  anecdote: The slave & the lion, 30-34
  definition, 17
  effect on animals, 29
  "free" among youths, 13

nonviolence is selfless, 25
tolerance is nature of, 26
unattainable without penance, 27
Manusmriti (scripture) on disciplined speech, 52
Masters
  realization of ultimate truth, 41
Meditation
  and the arousal of passion, 37-38
  nonviolence affects, 35-36
Mind
  affecting the subconscious, 36
  and passion, 37-38
  causing disturbance in another's, 64
  controlling unrestrained, 26, 35-36
  disturbances in dream state, 36
  meditation affected by disturbances, 36-38
  peace of essential to success, 55
  restraint of, 43
  spiritual discipline steadies, 66
  stability in sadhana, 35-38, 55
  stability indicates predominance of, 37
Nivritti path
  aids to practice of nonviolence, 37-38
  mind vs prana on, 36-38
  not for everyone, 63
  sadhak's battle with passion, 37-38
  See also Sahaj yoga
Niyamas. See also Yamas; Yamas & niyamas
Nonattachment (aparigraha), 69-80
  See also Attachment; Renunciation
  accomplished spontaneously by seeker of liberation, 74
  action in inaction best form of, 71
  anecdote: The laborer & the three stones, 80
  anecdote: The long-haired saint, 76-77
  anecdote: The mad saint, 77-80
  anecdote: The nonattached yogi Bhatrihari, 74-76
  anecdote: The old man & the mango tree, 69-70
  anecdote: The squirrel & the bridge, 72-74
  attained gradually, 69, 71, 80
  definition, 69
  selfless actions, stimulate growth of, 71
Nonstealing, 55-66
  See also Stealing
  definition, 56
Nonviolence (ahimsa), 23-38
  See also Violence
  aids to nivritti sadhak's practice of, 37
  anecdote: The slave & the lion, 30-34
  definition, 24, 35
  observation in sadhana, 35-38
  practice of inspires other virtues, 24
  seed of spiritual disciplines, 24
  three standards of, 35
  tolerance is expression of, 26
Passion
  arousal during meditation, 37-38
  Freudian concepts on, 5
  physical vs mental, 37-38
  yogis' views on, 5
Patanjali, Maharishi
  prescribed observance of yamas, 23
Prana
  awakens passion in sadhak, 37-38
  dependent vs independent, 36-37
  predominance causes instability of mind, 36-38
Pravritti path
  meditation & passion, 36-37

mind vs prana on, 36-37
practice of nonviolence on, 35-36
Purification
and the sadhak, 55
essential in yoga, 23
Restraint, sexual
conserves youthfulness, 10, 12
within marriage, 9-10
Rishi munis. See Sages, ancient
Sadhak
needs proper guidance, 77-78
purification, 55
sadhana & the mind of the, 55-56
See also Spiritual Seeker
Sadhana
Bapuji's suggestions to aid practice, 28-29
delusion constant obstacle in, 63
guidance of adept guru essential, 77-78
nonviolence observed according to type of, 35
required proper meditation, 55
revelation of esoteric truths in, 62-63
stability of mind essential in, 35
stages in, 35-37
three stages of, 35
violence in mind affects, 35-36
worldly is first stage to yoga, 26
yamas & niyamas protect, 23-24
Sages, ancient
scientific experiments with celibacy, 3-4
Sahaj yoga
sadhak's battle with passion, 36-38
See also Nivritti path
Saints
ordinary thieves are called, 56
Sanatan dharma, 52
Satya. See Truth
Science, spiritual
based on physical science, 3-4

definition, 4
recognizes experimental evidence of the guru, 4
Science, physical
source of spiritual science, 4
Scriptures
true vs deluded, 63
yogic experiences described in, 63
Seclusion
as aid to observing silence, 42
Secrets, yogic
concealed from understanding, 62-63
Seeker, spiritual
nonattachment & three types of, 69
See also Sadhak
Self-analysis. See Self-observation
Self-control. See Restraint
Self-defense. See Violence
Self-observation
Bapuji's practice of, 44
introspection progresses to, 44
seeker becomes sadhak as result of, 44-45
silence aid to, 44
Sex
proper attitude toward opposite, 10-12
Sexual energy
importance of conserving, 6-8
results of dissipating, 6-8
Sexual fluid
conserving, 7-8
internal secretion in child & yogi, 13
total sublimation evolves Divine Body, 13-14
Sexual restraint. See Restraint, sexual
Shankaracharyaji, Jagadguru
Indian ashram traditions re celibacy, 6
Shiva
anecdote: The nonattached yogi Bhatrihari, 74-76

Silence
  aid to obtain truth, 43
  aid to self-observation, 44
  anecdote: The businessman of Bengal—gramus & seclusion, 45-48
  Bapuji's observance of, 44
  discretion in speech vs total, 43-44
  power of, 43-44, 48
  purpose of observing, 35
Social service
  nonattachment & true, 69
Speech
  discrimination in, 48
  effects on family, 25-27
  great masters restrain, 48
  is manifest thought, 25
  Lord Shri Krishna's preachings on disciplined, 32
  practicing sweet, 26
  process of, 44
  restraint of, 43
  violence in, 25
Spiritual disciplines. See Disciplines, spiritual
Stealing
  anecdote: The angel & the hyena, 56
  as art in ancient India, 58
  anecdote: The theft of a cloth, 58-62
  definition, 62
  deities incarnate as thieves, 58
  disturbs mind, 56
  effects of single act of, 64
  everyone is a thief, 58
  form of violence, 64
  great yogis skillful in, 58
  some people justify, 56
  thoughts of others, 63-64
  types of thieves, 56
  See also Nonstealing
Stories (Bapuji's). See Anecdotes
Theft. See Stealing

Thief. See Stealing
Thoughts
  control of, 44
  effects of silence & seclusion on, 44
  effects on celibacy, 12
  expression of, 43-44
  impotent until channeled into behavior, 64
  integration with practice effects change, 27
  theft of, 63-64
  unmanifest speech, 25
  unverbalized speech, 44
  See also Mind; Chitta
Truth (Satya)
  aids to obtaining, 43,48
  avoidance & fear of, 41-42
  definition, 41
  discrimination in speech as step to, 48
  effect on others, 42
  effects on family, 41-42
  in speech, 41-42
  inner freedom inspires speaking, 41
  protected by yogis for deserving, 48-49
  silence aid to attain, 42-43
  vs. untruth, 41-42
Truth (Ultimate)
  masters' realization of, 41
Vice
  one attracts others, 24
Vinit Muni, 62
Violence
  apathy is seed of, 26
  disturbs mind, 35
  everyone tends toward, 25
  hatred extreme form of, 25
  in speech, 25-26
  intolerance manifests as, 26
  misconceptions about, 25
  objective vs subjective viewpoints, 24-25

self-defense for sadhaks, 36
selfish love best form of, 25
See also Nonviolence
Virtue
cultivating appreciation for, 28
one attracts others, 24
Virya. See Sexual fluid
Vow
of celibacy
Weapons
gross vs subtle, 25
Yamas (spiritual disciplines)
breaking disturbs the mind, 64, 66
celibacy, 3-20
nonattachment, 69-80
nonstealing, 55-66
nonviolence, 23-38
nonviolence seed of, 24
Patanjali's advice on, 23
truth, 41-52
See also Yamas & Niyamas; Niyamas
Yamas and niyamas
essential to practice of religion, 23
protect sadhana, 23
Yoga
aids & obstacles to, 23-24
as basis for celibacy experiments, 3
delusions in sadhana, 63
knowledge given as capacity develops, 62-63
purification essential to practice, 23
secrets concealed from undeserving, 62-63
spiritual science, 4
worldly sadhana first stage, 26
See also Sadhana; Disciplines, various types yoga
Yogi
conceals truth from undeserving, 62-63
most skillful thief, 58
scriptures written by deluded, 63
Youth. See Adolescents